EMINENT DOMAIN

RICHARD ELLMANN

EMINENT DOMAIN

YEATS
AMONG
WILDE
JOYCE
POUND
ELIOT
AND
AUDEN

New York OXFORD UNIVERSITY PRESS 1967

FOR PERMISSION TO REPRINT
PASSAGES FROM THE FOLLOWING WORKS GRATEFUL ACKNOWLEDGMENT IS MADE TO:

THE MACMILLAN COMPANY for "The Folly of Being Comforted" in *Collected Poems* by William Butler Yeats, copyright 1903 by The Macmillan Company, renewed 1931 by William Butler Yeats; for "Into the Twilight," "Who Goes with Fergus?" and "To Ireland in the Coming Times" in *Collected Poems* by William Butler Yeats, copyright 1906 by The Macmillan Company, renewed 1934 by William Butler Yeats; for "To A Child Dancing Upon the Shore" in *Collected Poems* by William Butler Yeats, copyright 1916 by The Macmillan Company, renewed 1944 by Bertha Georgie Yeats; for "In Memory of Major Robert Gregory" and "The Scholars" in *Collected Poems* by William Butler Yeats, copyright 1919 by The Macmillan Company, renewed 1946 by Bertha Georgie Yeats; for "Two Songs From a Play" and "The Tower" in *Collected Poems* by William Butler Yeats, copyright 1928 by The Macmillan Company, renewed 1956 by Georgie Yeats; for "Vacillation," "Byzantium," and "The Choice" in *Collected Poems* by William Butler Yeats, copyright 1933 by The Macmillan Company, renewed 1961 by Bertha Georgie Yeats; for "The Land of Heart's Desire," "Calvary," "The Countess Cathleen," and "Antigone" from *The Collected Plays of W. B. Yeats,* copyright 1934, 1952 by The Macmillan Company; for "An Acre of Grass," "The Gyres," "What Then?" "The Spur," and "Under Ben Bulben" in *Collected Poems* by William Butler Yeats. Copyright 1940 by Georgie Yeats.

THE VIKING PRESS, INC. for "The Holy Office" in *The Portable James Joyce.* All rights reserved; and from *A Portrait of the Artist as a Young Man* by James Joyce, copyright 1916 by B. W. Huebsch, 1944 by Nora Joyce, copyright © 1964 by the Estate of James Joyce.

NEW DIRECTIONS PUBLISHING CORPORATION for *Personae,* copyright 1926, 1954 by Ezra Pound; for *The Cantos,* copyright 1948 by Ezra Pound; for *The Classic Noh Theatre of Japan* by Ezra Pound and Ernest Fenollosa. Copyright © 1959 by New Directions. All rights reserved.

HARCOURT, BRACE & WORLD, INC. for "Little Gidding" in *Four Quartets,* copyright 1943 by T. S. Eliot; and for "A Cooking Egg" in *Collected Poems 1909-1962* by T. S. Eliot.

RANDOM HOUSE, INC. for *Selected Poetry of W. H. Auden,* copyright © 1958, by W. H. Auden; for *Homage to Clio,* copyright © 1960, by W. H. Auden, all rights reserved; for *Nones,* copyright © 1951, by W. H. Auden; and for *Ulysses,* by James Joyce, copyright 1914, 1918 by Margaret Caroline Anderson, copyright 1934 by The Modern Library Inc., copyright 1942, 1946 by Nora Joseph Joyce.

THE SOCIETY OF AUTHORS, London, as the literary representatives of the Estate of the late James Joyce, for *Stephen Hero,* copyright 1944 by New Directions, copyright © 1955, 1959, 1963 by New Directions.

CURTIS BROWN, LTD. for *Letters from Iceland* by W. H. Auden and Louis MacNeice, copyright 1937 by Faber and Faber, Ltd. All rights reserved. And for *Lions and Shadows* by Christopher Isherwood, copyright 1947 by New Directions.

HOLT, RINEHART AND WINSTON, INC. for *The Complete Poems of Robert Frost,* copyright 1934 by Holt, Rinehart and Winston, Inc., copyright © 1962 by Robert Frost.

TO

STEPHEN

MAUD

&

LUCY

Contents

EMINENT DOMAIN

I

—»» «««—

Introduction

'INFLUENCE' is a term which conceals and mitigates the guilty acquisitiveness of talent. That writers flow into each other like waves, gently rather than tidally, is one of those decorous myths we impose upon a high-handed, even brutal procedure. The behavior, while not invariably marked by bad temper, is less polite. Writers move upon other writers not as genial successors but as violent expropriators, knocking down established boundaries to seize by the force of youth, or of age, what they require. They do not borrow, they override.

Because Yeats declined to subside, like some writers, into addled repetitiveness, his conduct with the slightly older Oscar Wilde and then with the younger Joyce, Pound, Eliot, and Auden offers a history of eminent domain. Among poets he was one of the most generous, not so generous however as to fail to take over what he needed. Invited to dine with Oscar Wilde on Christmas day, 1888, he consumed not only his portion of the turkey but all Wilde's esthetic system, which Wilde read to him from the proofs of 'The Decay of Lying.' Once expropriated, this was developed and re-unified in Yeats's mind. If Yeats was quick to confiscate from Wilde, a reverse maneuver also occurred. As Wilde prepared his own fall, he read with admiration Yeats's story, 'The Crucifixion of the Outcast'; while in prison he obtained it again along with its companion stories of *The Secret Rose*; and in 'The Ballad of Reading Gaol' and 'De Profundis' he helped himself to some of Yeats's imagery of the noble malefactor.

What occurs then is not the assertion of a single sovereignty but of conflicting sovereignties which now encroach and now are encroached upon, like Italian city states in Malatesta's time. Yeats furnished Frank O'Connor with some good lines, then took over others from O'Connor for his own purposes. An impressively intricate example is provided by Ezra Pound. Initially Pound regarded himself as Yeats's disciple, then he sought to break with much of Yeats's teaching and to re-instruct his teacher. Yeats, having independently concluded that his style must be freshened, at first repudiated, then solicited Pound's help in the process of transformation. As his new manner evolved, however, he disavowed Pound's own solution of the problem.

With Joyce, Eliot, and Auden, Yeats was not at such close quarters as with Pound, but the same impingements upon each other's province took place. Joyce's decision to write prose rather than verse stemmed partly from his sense of Yeats's supremacy, but having surrendered a little he rebelled a good deal, objecting in hard prose to the soft attributes he found in Yeats—a sympathy with past beauty rather than with beauty yet undiscovered, a troubadour abasement in love, a nationalism more ardent than discriminating. But within this rebellion, poems which he accepted, from the poet he rejected, went through his mind so intensely that Joyce had to incorporate them in his own prose work, whether as respectful allusions or as targets for mockery. Yeats ingested less of Joyce, but sufficient to enlarge his notion of literary propriety, and the opening of his *Autobiography* suggests, in its epic fragmentation, that he had been reading the first pages of A *Portrait of the Artist as a Young Man*. As indeed he had.

When T. S. Eliot came to England and met Yeats, he kept his distance, the more easily because he was convinced that Yeats belonged to a different planet, even remoter than Ireland. But gradually the orbits of that planet and earth began to coincide in Eliot's mind; he allowed more and more merit in Yeats until, in 'Little Gidding,' he accepted him as wraith if not as living man. He paid him there the compliment—an ultimate one among poets—of appropriating for his own use Yeats's central images of fire and dance. As for Yeats, he made Eliot into a useful alter ego in 'An Acre of Grass,'

> Midnight, an old house,
> Where nothing stirs but a mouse,

only to have his Gerontion break down the walls which encased Eliot's. He countered *The Waste Land* in 'Lapis Lazuli,' drawing as Eliot had done upon Shakespeare, the cycles of civilization, and the East for his imagery, then overmastering despair with tragic gaiety.

Auden was not so tense as Eliot about Yeats; from the beginning he swept Yeats into his own consciousness, crossing that magnificence with his own gnomic plainness, offering to supplant Yeats's personal myth with an 'antimythological myth.' For his part, Yeats began in his last years to respond to Auden, as he had responded to Joyce, Pound, and Eliot; he encompassed in *The Herne's Egg* and *Purgatory* some of the clipped rhythm and intentionally awkward syntax which Auden had made available for confiscation.

Boundaries are scarcely drawn when they are violated, sometimes with collusion. Eliot and Pound encroached systematically upon each other. Pound found the structure of his *Hugh Selwyn Mauberley* (*Life and Contacts*) in *Prufrock and Other Obser-*

vations, so that he too began with a partly caricatured hero, pro-
ceeded to vignettes of the age and then of individuals, and
concluded with a somewhat ambiguous love poem. When he
began the *Cantos* he allowed Eliot (impinging now as critic)
to persuade him to break decisively with sequence, and then in
riposte persuaded Eliot to omit parts of *The Waste Land* and
thereby sharpen the discontinuous effect which Pound had pre-
viously assumed from Eliot.

The imposition of sovereignty over others' themes, vocabu-
laries, and metrical effects is not always so prosperous. The
nautical breeziness of Masefield's 'A Wanderer's Song,'

> Oh I am sick of brick and stone, the heart of me is sick,
> For windy green, unquiet sea, the realm of Moby Dick;
> And I'll be going, going, from the roaring of the wheels,
> For a wind's in the heart of me, a fire's in my heels,

cannot quite master the landsman's aspiration of 'The Lake
Isle of Innisfree,' the 'fire in my head' of 'The Song of Wandering Aengus,' or 'the creak of the lumbering cart' from 'The
Lover Tells of the Rose in His Heart.' A similar failure is
apparent in some poems of Robert Frost's first book, *A Boy's
Will.* Although Frost was eager later to deny having been influenced by any but American writers like Thoreau and Long-
fellow, plus that pre-American poet Horace, he had obviously
read Yeats intently and had encouraged his pupils to put on
two of Yeats's early plays. 'The Trial by Existence' shows Frost
still coping unsuccessfully with the problem of swallowing up
Yeats into his own work:

> And the awe passes wonder then,
>   And a hush falls for all acclaim.
> And God has taken a flower of gold
>   And broken it, and used therefrom
> The mystic link to bind and hold
>   Spirit to matter till death come.

The lines in Yeats which Frost found so indigestible were:

> Come, heart, where hill is heaped upon hill
> For there the mystical brotherhood
> Of sun and moon and hollow and wood
> And river and stream work out their will;
>
> And God stands winding his lonely horn,

Frosts's flower of gold emerging from 'the casket of gold' in Yeats's 'The Lover Tells of the Rose in His Heart.' This casket appears again in Frost's 'Love and a Question,'

> The bridegroom looked at the weary road,
>   Yet saw but her within,
> And wished her heart in a case of gold
>   And pinned with a silver pin,

the pin coming from 'He Gives His Beloved Certain Rhymes' after brief exchange with the silver and golden apples in 'The Song of Wandering Aengus.' The plan for Frost's A Boy's Will, published in Lawrance Thompson's biography, is modeled on the table of contents of The Wind among the Reeds.

Frost came to recognize that he could not encompass Yeats's elaborate manner, but he did better with Yeats's peasant diction. In a letter he quotes approvingly an unnamed friend who remarked that 'all the Masefield and Gibson sort of thing' could be derived from a line in The Land of Heart's Desire, 'The butter's at your elbow, Father Hart.' This and other illustrations of the art of sinking in Yeats, such as,

> It has been in the thatch for forty years.
> My father told me my grandfather wrote it,
> Killed a red heifer and bound it with the hide.
> But draw your chair this way—supper is spread,

seem also to underlie Frost's narrative poems, though he is not so limp. Then later, when Auden as a very young man writes,

> Someone cried, 'Look!': we crowded to the pane;
> Their tops still glittering from last night's rain
> They swayed a little, and upon their boughs
> Swung to and fro each black untidy house
> The rooks had made in some past century,
> And mended every springtime,

he is fumbling with an effort to superimpose himself upon Frost—a mode which he decided to give up.

In expropriating Yeats, as in expropriating Shakespeare, there is always the danger of not having sufficient strength. The greater the poet, the more resistant he is to being assimilated. So in recent work, we come upon such a passage as this one,

> I told him: the time has come, I must be gone.
> It is time to leave the circus and circus days,
> The admissions, the menagerie, the drums,
> Excitements of disappointment and praise.
> In a suburb of the spirit I shall seize
> The steady and exalted light of the sun,
> And live there, out of the tension that decays,
> Until I become a man alone of noon,

and realize that John Berryman in his youth could not establish sovereignty over images taken from 'The Circus Animals' Desertion' and 'The Tower,' or from Wallace Stevens's 'The Comedian as the Letter C.' The effect of reading Yeats on Theodore Roethke was much more seriously deleterious. Though he says boldly, 'I take this cadence from a man named Yeats,' it was Yeats who gradually took possession of Roethke's later verse.

Because language is common and literature is continuous, the words in a book are coded records of successive impositions of eminent domain. The best writers expropriate best, they disdain petty debts in favor of grand, authoritative larcenies.

II

※ ※

Oscar and Oisin

YEATS CAME to know Oscar Wilde during that period when he was obliged, and disposed, to respond to a new literary society. His family moved to London in April 1887, his twenty-first year. He could not afterwards regard Ireland in quite the same way. In Dublin he had made one of a company of young mystics, but these seemed virginal in comparison with the great hermeticists Madame H. P. Blavatsky and MacGregor Mathers whose orders he entered in London. In Dublin, nationalism was the movement to stir the hopes of the young, while in London this was three hundred years out of date and among young Englishmen anarchism and socialism had the cry. Writers like William Morris, whom Yeats quickly came to know, were more various than writers of his acquaintance in Dublin. Not that he succumbed to what he saw: his letters home, his 'dreamladen' poems and tales about the west, his editions of Irish poets and storytellers, his sense of himself as an Irish writer indicate how he clung to what, in a sense, he had left forever. His point of view could never again be simple, and for many reasons, not all of them conscious, he held just as hard, until late in life, to his rooms in Woburn Buildings near Euston Station. 'To an Irishman,' he explained, 'England is fairyland.' When Hugh Kings-

9

mill asked him if Wilde was not a snob, he gave an answer made indulgent by his own experience, 'No, I would not say that. England is a strange country to the Irish. To Wilde the aristocrats of England were like the nobles of Baghdad.'

Already settled in this Persian scene were, besides Wilde, two other literary compatriots, George Moore and Bernard Shaw, also a generation ahead of him. Moore was the most established, having won an audience with his early novels; Shaw and Wilde were still eyeing success. Both were none the less conspicuous on the London foam, Wilde in particular having been painted, caricatured, and parodied for a decade. Among the three, Yeats was to have most to do with Moore, though they met some years later. He met Shaw and Wilde at a time when he did not yet know his way.

The encounter with Shaw took place at William Morris's house, and was promptly recorded in Yeats's letters and in Shaw's journal. Yeats could not deny Shaw's wit but he could question Shaw's depth and consider him 'cold-blooded,' an estimate to which, in spite of many *pro forma* compliments, he afterwards kept. To Shaw, Yeats's interest in another world was an exploitation of Irish weaknesses, though he conceded later that Yeats 'was always careful not to act nor romance or otherwise try to impose on me as he did on his Rosicrucian fans.' It was quickly clear that the two were headed for a lifelong argument. But if Shaw, or for that matter Moore, had never lived, Yeats would have come round to the same view. Wilde, however, obtruded further into his consciousness.

In his *Autobiography* Yeats said that at the time of their first meeting, Wilde had already reviewed *The Wanderings of Oisin* and praised it without qualification. He was cavalier about time and attitude, the date being later, the attitude more reserved. His sense of Wilde's generosity improved a little upon the two reviews, kind as they were, which Wilde devoted to the book. They were grounded on Wilde's illusion that his own, and late nineteenth-century art in general, might alternate between the 'sunlit heights' of Athenian classicism and the Aeolian harp of English romanticism. Measuring Yeats accordingly, he found elements of both present, yet still inchoate; the title poem had something of the epic's largeness of vision but lacked the epic's grand simplicity. (It was still good enough for Wilde, in conversation, to compare Yeats's storytelling ability to Homer's.) Some of the poems were fragmentary and incomplete, lacking in that architectonic quality for which Matthew Arnold had made everyone look. As for the romantic temper, Wilde admired the blend of Celt and Keats, of 'very naïve and very primitive' ingredients along with richness and delicacy. On the other hand, he noted some danger of 'outglittering' Keats with 'strange crudities and irritating conceits.' He complained that Yeats was 'more fascinated by the beauty of words than by the beauty of metrical music,' a friendly way of noting a number of lapses in the latter. Yeats deferentially corrected these as soon as he could. Wilde also objected to the word 'populace' in the line,

And a small and feeble populace stooping with mattock and spade;

he said it was 'somewhat infelicitous.' Yeats changed it to 'race' for twenty years; then a certain amount of infelicity began to seem desirable to him, and he changed it back. Wilde, after registering these strictures, prophesied that Yeats would do work of 'high import.' He added shrewdly, 'Up to this he has been merely trying the strings of his instrument, running over the keys.' Yeats cannot have forgotten this remark, since when he in turn criticized the poems of the twenty-year-old Joyce in 1902, he wrote that they were 'the poetry of a young man who is practicing his instrument, taking pleasure in the mere handling of the stops.'

Before Wilde ceremoniously heralded Yeats's advent to London, the two men knew about each other through Lady Wilde, Oscar's mother. On 25 July 1888 she first invited Yeats to call, and after that he came often, to be greeted each time as 'My Irish poet.' He was delighted with 'Speranza's' revolutionary past and with her folklorist present, demonstrated the year before by her book *Ancient Legends, Mystic Charms and Superstitions of Ireland*. From it he was to borrow the wooden plot of his play, *The King's Threshold*. In his own *Fairy and Folk Tales of the Irish Peasantry*, published late in September 1888, he praised her book for divulging 'the innermost heart of the Celt in the moments he has grown to love through years of persecution, when, cushioning himself with dreams, and hearing fairy-songs in the twilight, he ponders on the soul and on the dead.' This praise was filially quoted by Wilde when he reviewed this book of Yeats as well.

In his *Autobiography* Yeats describes how he met Wilde first, not at Lady Wilde's house but at William Ernest Henley's. The place enables him to contrast Henley, busy and imperial, with Wilde, indolent and subversive. The time was evidently September 1888, for that was the month when Henley took up Wilde (he threw his stick at him later), and when Yeats referred to Wilde in a column for an American newspaper as 'the most finished talker of our time.' What made this first meeting 'an astonishment' was that Wilde spoke in perfectly formed sentences, unparalleled even among the eloquent Irishmen and Englishmen whom Yeats knew. The air he wore of having successfully assumed a new, rarefied personality (the opposite of the stage Irishman)—an effect enhanced by the likelihood that some of his conversation had been rehearsed—was for Yeats an allegorical victory of imagination over environment and heredity. He voiced something of this thought to Wilde, 'I envy those men who become mythological while still living,' and received in return a prescription for conduct, 'I think a man

should invent his own myth.' This remark of Wilde's is quoted
in the first draft of Yeats's *Autobiography*, and it is central to
his own views. Much of his work is a gloss on it, like his early
essay on Shakespeare which says that 'there is some one myth
for every man, which, if we but knew it, would make us under-
stand all he did and thought.' The sense of living a myth was
implicit in Yeats's defense of Wilde against the charge of being
a poseur; he told George Russell, an exponent of being true to
the depths of one's being, that posing 'was merely living artistically, and it was the duty of everybody to have a conception *self-*
of themselves, and he intended to conceive of himself.' Wilde's *begetting*
remark was in fact simmering in his mind, to be encompassed
into a system.

At Henley's, Wilde pleased Yeats also by his manner of com-
mending Pater's *Studies in the History of the Renaissance* to
that unPater-like company. 'It is my golden book,' he said, 'I
never travel anywhere without it; but it is the very flower of
decadence; the last trumpet should have sounded the moment
it was written.' 'But,' someone interjected, 'would you not have
given us time to read it?' and Wilde answered, 'Oh no, there
would have been plenty of time afterwards—in either world.'
Wilde was at once admiring Pater and making him faintly
ridiculous, freeing himself by professing outlandish bondage.
He did in fact regard Pater's style as too bookish, lacking 'the
true rhythmical life of words,' while Pater rejoined that Wilde's
style was too lifelike, that he wrote like an excellent talker.

Yeats's most memorable meeting with Wilde was on Christmas Day, 1888. Wilde invited him for dinner pretending that
Yeats was alone in London, a pretense Yeats was glad not to
embarrass by truth. Having heard the gossip about the untidy
house of Wilde's parents in Dublin, and about the dirty finger-
nails of Sir William Wilde, the eye-and-ear surgeon, he was un-
prepared for what he found in Tite Street. The drawing room

and dining room were done in white, not only the walls but furniture and rugs too. The only exception was the red lamp-shade suspended from the ceiling; this cowled a terra cotta statue which stood on a diamond-shaped red cloth in the middle of the white table. The effect of theatrical simplicity was like a Beardsley drawing.

There were, with all Wilde's suave goodwill, difficult moments. He started at his young visitor's shoes, which, like his poems, were found to be 'very naïve and very primitive' in their yellowness, a botched attempt to comply with the vogue for undyed leather. Yeats's effort to tell one of Wilde's children a story about a giant frightened the child to tears and earned a reproachful look from the father, whose own stories of giants dwelt upon their amiability rather than their monstrosity. Flustered by his gaucherie, Yeats was not wholly at a disadvantage. He knew that in poetry, the one kind of literature where Wilde had so far, by publishing a whole book, staked out a definite claim, his own powers were greater. Wilde's muscleless poetry was in fact an example of what not to do. 'Overshadowed by old famous men he could not attack, for he was of their time and shared their admirations,' Wilde had exaggerated 'every Victorian fault.' 'He thought he was writing beautifully when he had collected beautiful things and thrown them together in a heap. He never made anything organic while he was trying to be a poet.' Something of this verdict must have conveyed itself to Wilde at the Christmas dinner, for he converted the muted disparagement into articulate victory by saying, 'We Irish are too poetical to be poets; we are a nation of brilliant failures, but we are the greatest talkers since the Greeks.' This distinction Yeats was willing to allow, and he came to defend Wilde's best work as a kind of aristocratic oral literature, the educated counterpart of the oral tradition among the Irish peasantry. In keeping with this idea, he later, for the *Oxford Book of*

Modern Verse, pruned 'The Ballad of Reading Gaol' until it had lost almost all its 'foreign feathers' and was close to a folk ballad.

After dinner Wilde brought out the proofs of his essay, 'The Decay of Lying,' which was to be published the next month in the *Nineteenth Century*. It had an immediate and lasting effect on this first auditor. Yeats did not share the then fashionable aversion to critical theory, but until this time his own principal literary ideas were derived from occultism and nationalism. He needed an esthetic which would take account of the intense speculation about the nature and function of art that had been going on since the pronouncements of the romantic poets. This Wilde provided, summing up the disdain for experience of writers from Gautier to Mallarmé, the disdain for morality of Poe and Baudelaire, the disdain for content of Verlaine and Whistler. Wilde saw that such views might gather new vitality if counterposed against conventional theories of sincerity and verisimilitude. The most original aspect of his own essay came from its dialogue form, which enabled him to shift stance and emphasis as the conversation turned, sharpening the central paradox with all its dialectical possibilities.

As the title indicated, 'The Decay of Lying' began as a mockery of the current talk of Neronian decadence. Wilde spoke of a club called 'The Tired Hedonists,' and explained, 'We are supposed to wear faded roses in our buttonholes when we meet, and to have a sort of cult for Domitian.' To the suggestion that the members must be a good deal bored with each other, he agreed, 'We are. That is one of the objects of the club.' So Wilde smiled decadence away. He had also as target the essay by Zola published nine years before, *Le Roman expérimental*, which minimized imagination and style, and made the artistic labyrinth into a scientific laboratory. The true and lamentable decadence, Wilde said, was this Zolaesque encroachment of life upon art.

The esthetic he propounded was to be less ethical, less sal-
vationist than that of Matthew Arnold, whose recent death
seemed to give warrant to a new esthetician. Wilde accordingly
premised the superiority of the imagination to the faculties of
reason and observation. This being granted, then lies are better
than truths, whims than sobrieties, masks than faces. The truest
poetry is the most feigning. These opinions are developed in
Yeats's writings, for example, in his verse dialogue, 'Ego Dominus Tuus,' where Hic and Ille are very like Wilde's Cyril and
Vivian, one pleading for the self-realization that goes with sincerity and veracity, the other for the self-transcendence that
accompanies fabrication of a mask embodying all one is not. In
the poem, however, the discovery of what Yeats calls the anti-
self is the occasion for a sudden unleashing of energy; the anti-
self is more than a synthetic mask, it is a daimonic counterpart,
willed unconsciously as well as consciously, which when evoked
proves to have powers beyond those of the evoker. Wilde did
not present the fitting on of a mask as so culminative or preternatural; he thought of it as a kind of gambling with one's public
aspect rather than as a half-voluntary searching for a new being
with which the old being could fuse.

The preference for fabrication led Wilde to endorse the trend
of nineteenth-century painting toward Orientalism. The conventions of art should be so powerful as to envelop the work's
ostensible occasion. He joked about the vogue of Japan, saying
that 'the whole of Japan is a pure invention. There is no such
country, there are no such people.' While he was touting the
glory of art divorced from life, he was also adroitly mocking the
British disconnection from other cultures. Yeats shifted from
Japan to Byzantium: in the large, Byzantium too is a pure, or
at least an impure *invention*—a state of mind conjurable by an
ageing Irishman looking for a magnificent 'instead' for his own
and Western decrepitude. Japan and Byzantium are not areas

but conceits, the one propelling Wilde to witty excursions as
the other propelled Yeats to pernings in a gyre. Yeats pursued
the meaning of Orientalism more studiously: in half-Asiatic
Byzantium he saw an imaginative triumph of formalism over
random agitation, but in India he recognized something else, a
denial not only of life but of form as well: 'Grimalkin crawls to
Buddha's emptiness.' This renunciatory aspect of the East did
not interest Wilde; he liked Japanese painting rather than Sankara philosophy; for Yeats, however, Asia was capable of supply-
ing a continent-sized symbol of that will to erase, to demolish,
which he saw to be as native—at least latently—even in the
West, as the will to indite, to create.

Up to a point Wilde patronizes life for its inferiority to art,
but 'The Decay of Lying' has a second declension, which maintains that art inseminates life with its images. It brings color
to what would otherwise be neutral gray. 'Think of what we owe
to the imitation of Christ, of what we owe to the imitation of
Caesar.' Yeats kept this phrase in mind, quoting it in his *Autobiography*. It spurred him to two complications of the idea:
according to the first, history might be chronicled in terms of
the degree to which men's minds have been possessed by images
or have been dispossessed of them. In *Per Amica Silentia Lunae*
Christ and Caesar are masks worn by new actors, St. Francis and
Caesar Borgia:

> Some years ago I began to believe that our culture, with its
> doctrine of sincerity and self-realisation, made us gentle and
> passive, and that the Middle Ages and the Renaissance were
> right to found theirs upon the imitation of Christ or of some
> classic hero. Saint Francis and Caesar Borgia made them-
> selves overmastering, creative persons by turning from the
> mirror to meditation upon a mask.

In most subsequent considerations Yeats disjoined the Middle
Ages, which he saw as breaking down distinctions between men

and so attenuating their respective images, from the Renaissance, which magnified such distinctions and gave each its most defined expression.

Out of the same antithesis he framed a theory of psychological types. Men could be divided into two great categories, those who assumed and those who denied images. The first seek, through form, a means of control over 'mere anarchy,' the second practise submission, either by eliminating all deliberate effort or by accepting a 'passionate intensity' dictated by others. These contraries are spelled out in 'The Second Coming,' but they can be found much earlier, as in this draft of a passage for *The Player Queen*:

> Queens that have laughed to set the world at ease,
> Kings that have cried 'I am great Alexander
> Or Caesar come again' but stir our wonder
> That they may stir their own and grow at length
> Almost alike to that unlikely strength
> But those that will not make deliberate choice
> Are nothing or become some passion's voice
> Doing its will, believing what it choose.

The contrast is continued in later poems like 'A Dialogue of Self and Soul' and 'Vacillation,' though in them a *tertium quid*, a possible blending of these opposite urges within art, is envisaged.

Wilde was not capable of this rather Talmudic development of his own idea, and he was more concerned with the oscillation from Christ to Caesar than with putative reconciliations of them. He had at any rate enough to do in illustrating that men envisage the world in conformity with what artists have prescribed. Just as a geographical area may be considered a figment of the imagination, so with a temporal span: 'The nineteenth century, as we know it, is largely an invention of Balzac.' The word 'largely' is breezy enough to put down question. In a sentence greatly admired and often quoted by Proust, Wilde said,

'One of the greatest tragedies of my life is the death of Lucien de Rubempré.' Likewise Hamlet, though only a character in a play, has had his effect upon two centuries: 'The world has grown sad because a puppet was once melancholy.' Yeats cavilled at Wilde's lax substitution for 'sad' of 'melancholy,' and did not accept the defense that the sentence needed a full sound at the close; but he had no objection to the content. In 'The Gyres' he invokes and extends Wilde's epigram:

> Irrational streams of blood are staining earth;
> Empedocles has thrown all things about;
> Hector is dead and there's a light in Troy;
> We that look on but laugh in tragic joy.

Philosophers may affect the world as strongly as poets; Empedocles' image of the world as Strife was sealed by his suicide. He was himself like the volcano into which he plunged, and men and events could not choose but to break into hostile fragments in conformance with his view of them. The Trojan war was a historical event, but history can do nothing except offer its detailed confirmation of the power of imagination over life.

Wilde applied this theory of art as first cause to other arts besides literature. Corot's paintings created the fogs that they were thought merely to depict, an idea which Proust echoed when he said women began to look like Renoir's images of them. As for sculpture, Wilde said, 'The Greeks ... set in the bride's chamber the statue of Hermes or Apollo, that she might bear children as lovely as the work of art she looked at in her rapture or her pain. They knew that Life gains from Art not merely spirituality ... but that she can form herself on the very lines and colours of art, and can produce the dignity of Pheidias as well as the grace of Praxiteles.' To Yeats the images are not only cosmetic but, in their effects, military. As he writes at the end of his life in *On the Boiler*, 'Europe was not born when

Greek galleys defeated the Persian hordes at Salamis, but when
the Doric studios sent out those broad-backed marble statues
against the multiform, vague, expressive Asiatic sea, they gave
to the sexual instinct of Europe its goal, its fixed type.' This
classical world is much more Dionysian than Wilde had conceived it.

The principal theme in 'The Decay of Lying' develops from
overturning the conception of imitation. That art is an imitation of life, that life is an imperfect imitation of a supernal
world of forms, were theories of famous men which Wilde was
ready to revise. By his lights Plato had needlessly suggested that
the forms were extraterrestrial, when in fact they were terrestrial,
and could be found in the world of art. Art makes life imitate
it. Whether the forms of art have any source or sanction beyond
the human Wilde chose not to consider, sensing that metaphysical speculation would land him back in the romantics'
camp. In modifying Plato's cave he does some dexterous side-
stepping:

> Remote from reality, and with her eyes turned away from the
> shadows of the cave, Art reveals her own perfection, and the
> wondering crowd that watches the opening of the marvellous
> many-petalled rose fancies that it is its own history that is
> being told to it, its own spirit that is finding expression in a
> new form. But it is not so. The highest art rejects the burden
> of the human spirit, and gains more from a new medium or
> a fresh material than she does from any enthusiasm for art,
> or from any lofty passion, or from any great awakening of the
> human consciousness. She develops purely on her own lines.

Wilde allows art to take up the burden of neither the divine
nor the human spirit. The 'many-petalled rose' which festoons
the passage is an image that might imply some transcendent
origin, but is not allowed to do so; when Wilde speaks of the
'highest' art he associates it with a change of technique, not of

content or aspiration. We have grown accustomed today to what was then still unfamiliar doctrine, that new methods bring new meanings.

Just here Yeats asserted himself. With great self-restraint he did not take over the image of the rose, though he used it often in his verse; instead he assimilated from Rossetti an image equally rusty and romantic, but solider sounding: 'The beryl stone was enchanted by our fathers that it might unfold the pictures in its heart, and not to mirror our own excited faces, or the boughs waving outside the window.' He agrees with Wilde that art is neither confessional nor photographic, neither wholly subjective nor wholly objective. The beryl stone is what he usually calls Anima Mundi, a sublime lexicon of the imagination which stores old images and the potentialities of new ones. From it men draw, without necessarily meaning to, the models for their creations, creations which may be deeds as well as works of art. Because images give direction to conduct as well as to artifice, Yeats was able in *A Vision* to conceive of human destiny as a panorama of images and men, sometimes mixed congenially, sometimes not. At moments men achieve more or less reality because they are more or less at one with their images, incarnating or failing to incarnate. One of the great subjects of art becomes the tension of this relation, and another is the remission of tension either by total embodiment, or by an Asiatic rejection of all images, though Yeats sometimes implies that such a rejection is itself an imaginative feat.

Yeats needed the word symbolism to bind together particular symbols in the larger lexicon. Wilde spoke occasionally about symbols but had no interest in the kind of integration which Yeats developed. He did, however, dwell upon the way that symbols may lose as well as gain power over us, and said that they were 'as limited in extent and duration as the forces of physical energy.' Because Wilde conceived of the images as discontinuous rather than, as Yeats announced, processional, he thought life to be by nature dilettantism. When Yeats offers the same idea,

> Love's pleasure drives his love away.
> The painter's brush consumes his dreams,

it is to suggest a common source for both creation and destruction. Nonetheless, he was quick to see possibilities in Wilde's conception. One day Wilde said he had been inventing a new Christian heresy. Christ was crucified but did not die, and after burial managed to escape from his tomb. He lived on as a carpenter, the one man upon earth who knew the falsehood of Christianity. Once St. Paul visited his town and he alone in the carpenters' quarter did not go to hear him preach. Henceforth the other carpenters noticed that, for some unknown reason, he kept his hands covered. Yeats's mind smouldered with this fable for twenty years before he exalted it into his poem, "The Magi,' where not Christ but 'the pale unsatisfied ones' suffer from the diminution of an image that once possessed them.

Another fable, which Wilde called the best short story in the world, impressed Yeats also with its 'terrible beauty.' Christ came from a white plain to a purple city, and as he passed through the first street, he heard voices overhead, and saw a young man lying drunk upon a window-sill, 'Why do you waste your soul in drunkenness?' He said, 'Lord, I was a leper and You healed me, what else can I do?' A little further through the town he saw a young man following a harlot, and said, 'Why do you dissolve your soul in debauchery?' and the young man answered, 'Lord, I was blind, and You healed me, what else can I do?' At last in the middle of the city he saw an old man crouching, weeping upon the ground, and when he asked why he wept, the old man answered, 'Lord, I was dead and You raised me into life, what else can I do but weep?' From Yeats's point of view this grief was too diffuse—he didn't like weeping in art anyway—so when he took over Lazarus for his play *Calvary* he dried up the tears and replaced luxuriance in sorrow with truculence:

> For four whole days
> I had been dead and I was lying still
> In an old comfortable mountain cavern
> When you came climbing there with a great crowd
> And dragged me to the light.

Lazarus is in rebellion against Christ's love, and he exhibits a homely desire to live and die on his own terms. In the same play Judas is represented as betraying Christ not for gain but for freedom from God's power and mercy. Out of Wilde's promptings Yeats framed a battle between secular efflorescence and spiritual constriction, between the pluralism of images in life and art, and the imageless monism of religion. It is Anima Hominis, not Anima Dei, which he serves as prophet, though the other is a necessary countersign.

Wilde's most sustained retelling of a Biblical episode, *Salome*, dealt with his theme of spent images. The legend had been much worked by writers in France, but Wilde borrowed brazenly, knowing that it would assume a different expression through his mind. His old antithesis of Christ and Caesar appears here as John the Baptist against Herod and Salome, all three aroused by strange loves. Their ardors, sacred and profane, are strident. The first turns John into a sterile scold, the second turns Herod into a fool, Salome into a necrophile. Wilde's quite astringent theme is that their respective excesses, of renunciation and self-indulgence, are equally repulsive and ill-starred. There was much in this play for Yeats to dislike: he found the dialogue 'empty, sluggish, and pretentious,' and the action lacking in tension. He went reluctantly to a performance of it in 1905 and afterwards wrote a friend, 'The

audience was curiously reverential, and as I came away I said
to somebody, "Nothing kept us quiet but the pious memory
of the sainted author." ' On the other hand, he wrote a friend
in 1911 that *Salome* was very much a part of our time, and in
the 1930s he reconsidered it in *The King of the Great Clock
Tower* and later in *A Full Moon in March*. He replaced the atmosphere of morality and immorality alike gone fetid with a
quite energetic notion of 'the slain god, the risen god.' The
poet's head is severed but still sings because, in Auden's words,
the death of the poet is kept from his poems, or, in language
more like Yeats's, because images fructified by human passions
survive physical destruction, their human embodiments being in
fact temporary residences for animators more than human in
origin and strength. Here as elsewhere, Yeats imposed a metaphysical dimension, which could be called imaginative though
he, like Blake, considered *imaginative* a synonym for *eternal*,
upon Wilde's less haunted scene. For Yeats the preternatural is
enwoven with the natural. He imposed also a systematic symbolism upon what Wilde left improvisatory. A difference in temperament prevented his sharing Wilde's interest in the *failings*
of character; Yeats's personages are always gathering strength,
even when misguided. So *Salome* was reconstructed to make the
king strong, the queen profound, the poet-prophet right.

At the time that Wilde's fame turned to infamy, he came
himself to constitute a kind of image of the abused artist. His
career was, he thought, as archetypal as Byron's. Yeats was entirely in accord with what he regarded as Wilde's decision not
to escape, since escape would only blur the image. At the same
time, the passage from scapegrace to scapegoat was not altogether simple for Wilde. 'Even when disaster struck him down,'
Yeats said, 'it could not wholly clear his soul.' Though on release from prison Wilde promised to redeem his name, 'his heart
was shallow.' Yeats summed it up in a note after Wilde's death,

'He was an unfinished sketch of a great man.' The 'good things'
in his works are mostly lifted from his conversation, where he
could test them by immediate reaction. Avid for applause, he
moved from emphasis to emphasis. What was best in him
stemmed from a recklessness which Yeats compared to that of
an Irish eighteenth-century rake or gambler, or to 'an audacious
Italian fifteenth-century figure.' Only in *The Importance of
Being Earnest* did he completely accept this quality in himself
and so achieve, for the first time, unity.

As Wilde gained and then lost his public, Yeats struggled
toward his own position. He elaborated the esthetic theories
Wilde had imparted to him, and nourished the images. But
he also began to regard himself as belonging to a brother-
hood of symbolists as well as of occultists and patriots. There
were other esthetic theories around him, but they lacked solidity.
Walter Pater's impressionism was one of these; whatever its
usefulness in painting, when applied to literature it attached too
much value to what Yeats disliked as 'isolated lyrical moments.'
Another theory, decadence, was for a time espoused by Arthur
Symons, with whom Yeats shared rooms in the middle 'nineties.
Symons spoke of decadence warmly as 'really a new and beautiful and interesting disease,' and, in an essay on 'The Decadent
Movement in Literature' (1893), he exalted it until it sounded
like health: 'To fix the last fine shade, the quintessence of
things, to fix it fleetingly, to be a disembodied voice, and yet
the voice of a human soul: that is the ideal of Decadence.'
Yeats felt that this was a fainthearted and precious miscon-
ception. In 1898 he declared that what many called 'the decadence' he, because he believed 'that the arts lie dreaming of
things to come,' preferred to call 'the autumn of the flesh.' To
Symons's notion that decadence might be considered the trunk
of modern literature, and impressionism and symbolism its two
branches, Yeats responded that the trunk was symbolism. He

had spent three years, from 1892 to 1895, in bringing Blake's
symbolic system out of its supposed eccentricity and into the
main stream of European culture. Then, for Symons's magazine
The Savoy, he wrote three essays on Blake, relating him to
Mallarmé and Villiers de l'Isle-Adam, and offering a theory of
symbolist art. He contributed to *The Savoy* also his stories, 'The
Tables of the Law' and 'Rosa Alchemica,' in which the narrator
declares that for his mind 'symbolism was a necessity,' and also
several ostentatiously symbolic poems like 'The Secret Rose.'
Under this pressure, reinforced by much discussion in the
rooms they shared in Fountain Court, Symons had to change
his theory. He decided to publish a book on *The Symbolist
Movement in Literature* instead of on the decadent movement
as he had planned. Instead of being all decay, it was all re-
crudescence. This was one of the swiftest changes of face in
literary history. Appropriately the book was dedicated to Yeats.

Symons's book drifted genially among various interpretations
of symbolism, and had minimal force as a literary polemic. Yeats
wanted to declare himself emphatically, and he did so in 1900
in an essay entitled 'The Symbolism of Poetry.' He began by
defending the value of an esthetic, corroborating here Wilde's
essay on 'The Critic as Artist.' Then, after discussing the in-
definable symbolism in style, he took up the theme of the
relation of art to life, trying to anatomize more precisely the
way in which symbols, emotional and intellectual, gather their
force and spread their influence throughout the world:

> A little lyric evokes an emotion, and this emotion gathers
> others about it and melts into their being in the making of
> some great epic; and at last, needing an always less delicate
> body, or symbol, as it grows more powerful, it flows out, with
> all it has gathered, among the blind instincts of daily life,
> where it moves a power within powers, as one sees ring
> within ring in the stem of an old tree. This is maybe what
> Arthur O'Shaughnessy meant when he made his poets say

they had built Ninevah with their sighing; and I am certainly never sure, when I hear of some war, or of some religious excitement, or of some new manufacture, or of anything else that fills the ear of the world, that it has not all happened because of something that a boy piped in Thessaly. . . . I doubt indeed if the crude circumstance of the world, which seems to create all our emotions, does more than reflect, as in multiplying mirrors, the emotions that have come to solitary men in moments of poetical contemplation.

The statement is tender in a way that Yeats later would not have permitted, but with all its gracious qualifications it insists, as strongly as Wilde and with more subtlety, on the conception of life modeling itself upon art 'as in multiplying mirrors.' Here Yeats has poets alone in command of symbols, but in his later work heroes, as artists of action, may also be in command of them, as may lovers. We cannot fail to be symbolists to some degree. The material world is not solid but molten, with symbols in various states of realization.

This essay, published just before Queen Victoria's death, consolidates the esthetic thinking of Wilde and Yeats and, with whatever caution or freedom it was reinterpreted, summons into being such writers as Eliot, for whom the unreality of the modern city derives from its loss of animating images, or Pound, whose *Cantos* offer unexpected substitutes such as Confucius and Malatesta for the images of Christ and Caesar, or Wallace Stevens, who finds like Wilde that 'life is the reflection of literature.' Long after Wilde had passed out of fashion, he was still fulfilling indispensably the role of precursor.

III

⊰⊱

The Hawklike Man

IN THE IRISH literary movement the two principals, Yeats and Joyce, play complicated roles. Yeats serves as founder but then, as the movement progresses, he appears to be thinking of something else. Joyce is first the rebel, then the outcast of the movement, resentful of neglect yet more cheerful in his writing than might be anticipated. It is the gregarious Yeats who organizes the literary societies and theatre but whose poetry, even when it uses local and national themes, longs for 'a place of stone' apart from Dublin, and Joyce who exiles and isolates himself only to make his subject Dublin and a congress of men. Joyce rooted his work in natural acts as intently as Yeats in esoteric experience. Yet the arc of each man was wide enough to include the other, and neither escaped the other's gravitational pull.

Even in adolescence Joyce recognized that Yeats was the writer with whom he must finally compete. By the late 1890s, when Joyce was studying at University College, Dublin, Yeats was the acknowledged leader of what was already being called a literary revival. His difficulties were multiplying, however, for the nationalism he espoused was indifferent to immediate politics and put many patriots off, while his religious eclecticism grated on the more devout of his potential adherents. To fore-

stall tension, Yeats had encouraged impartially Catholics and
Protestants; he had made a point of writing for magazines of
both faiths. His poetic imagery incorporated Christian symbols
but without credal endorsement. In *The Celtic Twilight* (1893),
with what Joyce later described as 'delicate scepticism,' he
mingled fairies and angels, showing how country people in
the west of Ireland could appeal to the Trinity while at the
same time deferring to the pantheon of 'Celtic Heathendom.'
The stories of *The Secret Rose* (1897), set in an earlier
time, displayed a clash between the two dispensations, with
druids usually behaving more nobly than their enemies, the
priests. Yeats celebrated Oisin's wanderings (1889) against
Patrick's chastenings. Sometimes, as in 'The Tables of the Law'
and 'The Adoration of the Magi' (1897), he went so far as to
depict the coming of a new god to replace the incumbent.
While these notions were common enough among occultists
and comparative mythologists—to each eon its own avatar suited
Madame Blavatsky's thought, and the migratory routes of gods
were Frazer's theme in *The Golden Bough*—many of Yeats's
readers were not at home with them. His publishers, Lawrence
& Bullen, worried over possible repercussions, held over the
stories from *The Secret Rose*, and at last published them separately in a small edition which specified no publisher at all.

Joyce picked up the little book containing the two stories at
a bookstall on the quays. He learned 'The Tables of the Law'
by heart. There Yeats expounded, or rather expanded, the historical theories of Joachim of Flora, pretending that Joachim's
supposititious *Eternal Gospel* had been found. Joachim's conception of history was probably the first Joyce came to know
well, and it bore a relation, in its use of three ages succeeding
each other by shock, to the Viconian cycle which impressed him
so much, when he came upon it in Trieste, that he reserved it
for the structure of *Finnegans Wake*. According to Joachim the

ages of the Father and of the Son were now over, and that
of the Holy Spirit was about to begin. This age, like its prede-
cessors, would be ushered in by turbulence; antichrists would
appear, unconscionable acts of violence take place. Bad as these
were in themselves, they were yet necessary to mark out the
new age. A spiritual elite would now reveal the hidden substance
of God. Joachim had in mind a group of monks, but Yeats,
following Wilde's principle of the convertibility of religious and
artistic currencies—a principle that Joyce also accepted—inter-
preted the elite to be poets.

In 1899 Joyce had an occasion to defend this elite and Yeats
in particular. The Irish Literary Theatre was in progress of
formation, with Yeats's play *The Countess Cathleen* inaugurat-
ing it on 8 May. This play combined a variant of the Faust
legend with Irish history in a half-Christian phase. Pagan
notions attract the countess's attendant bard, Aleel, who has
to be admonished, 'These are no thoughts for any Christian
ear.' In selling her soul to the devil so as to rescue her people
from famine, Cathleen parallels the artist who undoes his soul
for the benefit of what Joyce called his 'wretched race.' The
countess goes to heaven rather than to hell on the theological
ground that God 'looks always on the motive, not the deed.'
The suspicion that some new moral code was at work here out-
raged much of the audience; while they hissed, Joyce clapped.
The next day a petition was circulated at his university, protesting the caricature of the Catholic peasantry. Joyce refused
to sign it. The student magazine castigated him as the only
student to withhold his signature, an accusation that Joyce
cherished as a badge of honor.

Although he was already responsive to the work of a very
different playwright, Ibsen, Joyce was none the less stirred by
The Countess Cathleen. Its effect can be seen in his works. In
1911, with a friend's help, he translated it into Italian, only to

have Yeats object to the version used, which was probably the
one Joyce had seen performed. Joyce pays Yeats the compliment
of quotation: in A *Portrait of the Artist as a Young Man*
Stephen remembers the countess's dying speech,

> Bend down your faces, Oona and Aleel,
> I gaze upon them as the swallow gazes
> Upon the nest under the eave before
> He wander the loud waters,

and blends it with his own images of flight and departure to
continental (rather than eternal) life. By the time of *Ulysses*,
while Stephen still likes to quote Aleel's song, 'Who Goes with
Fergus?'

> And no more turn aside and brood
> Upon Love's bitter mystery;
> For Fergus rules the brazen cars,
> And rules the shadows of the wood,
> And the white breast of the dim sea. . . .

Joyce admits the quotation less reverently. He has Bloom overhear a few of these words from Stephen, who has been knocked
down in Nighttown, and has him comment: 'Face reminds me
of his poor mother. In the shady wood. The deep white breast.
Ferguson, I think I caught. A girl. Some girl. Best thing could
happen him. . . .' In Bloom's confusion of King Fergus and the
even more fabulous Miss Ferguson, Joyce suspends Yeats's lines
in new, comic patterns of his own.

The young Joyce allowed only a short time for unequivocal
admiration. He soon diverged from Yeats over theatre policy.
The original plans of the new theatre proposed, with ambitious
vagueness, to produce European as well as Irish plays. For Joyce
this adjective could only mean Ibsen. Yeats, while averse to
naturalism and scarcely tolerant of prose drama, was still willing
to countenance Ibsenism when applied to Irish materials, and

he encouraged Edward Martyn to write plays of a Norwegian
cast. Joyce did not feel that these were limitless enough: he
wanted Ireland to be a part of Europe, while Yeats feared special qualities might thereby be lost. The insularity which repelled Joyce was to Yeats, if properly maintained, a source of
intensity. Their positions can be seen in relation to the movement for the revival of the Irish language—Joyce opposing and
Yeats sponsoring it, both thereby exempted from studying it.

Douglas Hyde's Irish version of Yeats's story, *The Twisting
of the Rope*, was accordingly fixed upon as curtain raiser for
the October 1901 performances of the Irish Literary Theatre.
The principal play was to be *Diarmuid and Grania* by Yeats
and George Moore. To Joyce both seemed drowned in archaic
legend, far from modern life. Without having read the longer
play, he guessed what outlines it must follow. The love story
of Diarmuid and Grania is as practical as it is romantic, and
neither Yeats nor Moore ever sought to publish their collabora-
tive version of it. One obstacle is the ambiguity of the conduct
of Grania, who leaves Finn MacCumhal, to whom she is
affianced, and lives with Diarmuid, only to return to Finn after
Diarmuid's death. In the comparable story of Deirdre, the
heroine has the grace to die rather than move about so easily.
'What Morals, if any, can be drawn from Diarmuid and
Grania?' is proposed as a thin subject for a schoolboy theme in
Finnegans Wake. But whatever its Aristotelian limitations as
tragedy, Joyce found of some interest the character of Finn,
whose patriarchal lubricity serves Humphrey Chimpden Earwicker later as an antecedent.

Before the new plays had been put on, Joyce divined their
quality from their titles, and turned out his attack, 'The Day of
the Rabblement,' for the college magazine. After a rejection
there he had it printed and distributed privately. His Ibsenism
was now in full cry: the theatre must liberate people from

spiritual bondage, or surrender to the 'trolls' of mediocrity and repression. The new plays had surrendered to nationalistic vulgarity: 'The Irish Literary Theatre must now be considered the property of the most belated race in Europe.' Frank Fay attempted to answer this charge in the *United Irishman* of 2 November 1901, by arguing rather feebly that the production of a play in Irish could scarcely be considered a pandering to the English-speaking populace.

In 'The Day of the Rabblement' Joyce took up the various Irish dramatists in turn. His tone with Yeats was magnificently lofty: 'It is equally unsafe at present to say of Mr. Yeats that he has or has not genius. In aim and form *The Wind among the Reeds* is poetry of the highest order, and *The Adoration of the Magi* (a story which one of the great Russians might have written) shows what Mr. Yeats can do when he breaks with the half-gods. But an aesthete has a floating will, and Mr. Yeats's treacherous instinct of adaptability must be blamed for his recent association with a platform [the Irish language movement] from which even self-respect should have urged him to refrain.' Yeats gave no indication of having received the pamphlet, although it was delivered by hand to his door, but in a letter written to Joyce a year later he listed among the indispensable attributes of a writer the quality of 'adaptability,' and added, in dry parenthesis, 'without this one learns nothing.'

That Joyce confined his praise of Yeats's poetry to 'aim and form' suggests a reservation about content. Long afterwards, in talking with Austin Clarke, he described Yeats's early verse as being like the verse of Mangan, 'the poetry of onanism.' Probably he had this idea in mind when, in an early passage of *Finnegans Wake*, he imagined St. Kevin as sequestering himself within a 'lake-isle,' inside a 'beehut.' Onanism was not necessarily disqualifying, however, for Joyce set several of the poems to music and sang them to his friends. The fact is that he shared with Mangan and the early Yeats a liking for hypnotic undulations of language.

As for Joyce's criticism of the stories, his statement that 'The Adoration of the Magi' was Russian indicates that he read it almost literally, as a destruction of the past and an inception of the future. (Yeats returned the compliment in 1915 by saying, with more justice, that *Dubliners* had a Russian quality.) The three old men who receive the revelation of a new era from the dying woman subdivide into a quaternion in the apocalyptic apparatus of Joyce's story 'Grace' and then of *Finnegans Wake*. Like many of his youthful attitudes, Joyce's disrespect for parochialism would later be modified: 'To me an Irish safety-pin,' he told a friend in 1918, 'is more important than an English epic.' But whatever the modifications afterwards, the pamphlet is free of misgivings; nineteen years old, Joyce was determined to be patronizing rather than patronized.

He grew, in fact, rapidly confident of his powers as a writer, and not averse to suffering their public confirmation. So in 1902 he decided to show his work to the leading literary men of Dublin. With the industry of narcissism, he bought large pieces of parchment and copied verses on to them in an elegant hand. He would indulge this happy hobby in later years as well. If he sought to give weight to his criticism, Joyce sought for his poetry weightlessness, a quality which it unfortunately achieves. He moved away from Yeats by not attempting a many-layered symbolism, by not making the beloved a Dantean symbol binding heaven and earth but a more cajolable entity; love becomes a romantic convention so exhausted as to be slightly undermined. Like other Irish and English poets of the time, he could not quite keep away from the vocabulary which Yeats had virtually patented, so that words like 'dew,' 'pale,' and 'light footfall' often intrude, though in contexts less ponderable than Yeats's.

Joyce copied out also his prose epiphanies, those *Ur*-Happenings in which circumstances were made to flash out their meanings. He wisely came armed with both poems and prose for his meetings with Dublin writers. His first choice was George Russell, known to be accessible and helpful to the young. Showing a keener sense of drama than of consideration, Joyce arrived late at night, apologetic but importunate. Admitted, he talked for a time, dazzling and intimidating by such maneuvers as quoting Ibsen in the original to the monolingual Russell. He then displayed some of his epiphanies, accepting praise without visible emotion. He stayed until four o'clock in the morning. Yet, if the evidence of *Ulysses* can be trusted, he was not pleased to hear afterwards that Russell had told 'some Yankee interviewer' how the young man 'came to him in the small hours of the morning to ask him about planes of consciousness.' The subject was certainly one to engross him—he later commended T. S. Eliot's phrase 'two-plane' to describe the method of *Ulysses*—but he preferred his friends to think that in engaging Russell on Theosophy he was playing some deep prank. Though genuinely curious, he equated intellectual search with vulnerability. Yet he pursued the matter in Sinnett's *Esoteric Buddhism*, and he continued to mull over such themes as historical periodicity, the soul's urge to repeat its pattern in a new body, and the reductibility of existence to certain unchanging laws. Stanislaus Joyce says his brother was looking for a transitional faith, but since James soon declared himself 'incapable of any belief'—that in his own soul excepted—he was evidently looking for a way to extend that soul atemporally as well as internationally.

The interview understandably jarred Russell; he at once wrote Lady Gregory that Yeats had succeeded in evoking the first of a new race and, he implied, might live to regret it. He next communicated directly with Yeats: 'I want you very much to

meet a young fellow named Joyce whom I wrote to Lady
Gregory about half jestingly. He is an extremely clever boy
who belongs to your clan more than to mine and more still to
himself. But he has all the intellectual equipment, culture and
education, which all our other clever friends here lack. And I
think writes amazingly well in prose though I believe he also
writes verse and is engaged in writing a comedy which he expects
will occupy him five years or thereabouts as he writes slowly.
Moore who saw an article of this boy's ['The Day of the Rabblement'] says it is preposterously clever. Anyhow I think you
would find this youth of 21 with his assurance and self-confidence
rather interesting.' So within a few days in August 1902, Joyce's
presence in Dublin was felt by Russell, Yeats, Lady Gregory,
and Moore, as if to demonstrate the advantages of a small
capital.

His meeting with Yeats took place shortly after his meeting
with Russell. Like most Dublin encounters, this one was bi-
nomial, comprised of what was actually said and what was afterwards bruited. Rumor made Joyce tell Yeats flatly, 'You are
too old for me to help you.' Later both men declared publicly
that the remark had not been made, while privately they conceded that, at least approximately, it had been. In a middle-aged
disclaimer dictated for his biographer Herbert Gorman, Joyce
attested that 'though he did say the words or something to the
effect attributed to him they were never said in the tone of con-
tempt which is implied in the story. . . . The whole point of the
remark so far as he can remember was that the elder poet had
grown up in an earlier aesthetic atmosphere (William Morris
etc.) in which the younger had no part.' What this means may
be deduced from a distorted version of the remark which Joyce
introduced into *Finnegans Wake:* 'I have met with you, bird,
too late, or if not, too worm and early.' Evidently he had not
offered to *help* Yeats.

The meeting impressed itself on Yeats, and he retained from
it a permanent image of a brilliant but cruel mind. He wrote
down a summary of their talk with the idea that it might serve
as preface to his essays, *Ideas of Good and Evil* (1903), but in
the end he omitted it, not wishing to start the book off in so
defensive a posture. The unused preface, some other notes, and
a comment in his *Autobiography* reconstitute much of what
was said between them. Joyce, eager to display both his art and
his theories of art, began by reading aloud his epiphanies; he
prefaced them with the explanation, calculated to put off a lyric
poet, that he 'had thrown off metrical form that he might get
a form so fluent ... it would respond to the motions of the
spirit.' Yeats praised them, probably without expressing the
reservation he felt and wrote later, that they 'were a beautiful
though immature and eccentric harmony of little prose descriptions and meditations.' Joyce responded with the same coolness
he had manifested to Russell, 'I really don't care whether you
like what I am doing or not. It won't make the least difference
to me. Indeed I don't know why I am reading to you.'

In terror of excessive charm, Joyce next took up his objections
to Yeats's recent work. Yeats does not specify which work, but
the objections seem directed against his new play *Cathleen ni
Houlihan*, which had scored such a success in April that it was
to be produced again in October. It was set in 1798, the time
when the French landed at Killala to spur an Irish revolt; Joyce
severely criticized the historical setting of events in drama. The
title character was a grandiloquent remnant of folklore, and
folklore was too imaginatively enfeebled to have authority. The
play's theme was political and so extraneous to genuine art.
In sum, Joyce accused Yeats of falling victim to inartistic generalizations, a sign, he said, of the cooling of the iron, of the
fading out of inspiration.

These strictures were accompanied by an engaging smile and

the remark, 'I am not as you see treating you with deference, for after all both you and I will be forgotten.' Modest as Yeats was, he was pricked enough to justify himself. The folk, he contended, were close to the source of inspiration. Joyce pointed to his epiphanies; these owed nothing to folklore or indeed to anything but his own mind, which he said was closer to God than folklore. For answer Yeats pointed to a passage in one of the epiphanies, 'You got that from somebody else who got it from the folk.' Then, warming to his theme, he insisted that a writer schooled in urban elegancies must take violent measures to overcome sterile sophistication. As he phrased the problem a little later, 'I could not get away ... from images and dreams which had all too royal blood, for they were descended like the thought of every poet from all the conquering dreams of Europe, and I wished to make that high life mix into some rough contemporary life without ceasing to be itself, as so many old books and plays have mixed it and so few modern....' He had lent his ear methodically to the peasants of Aran and Galway, and had instigated Lady Gregory and Synge to do likewise. Through a marriage of town and country, of deliberate artistic idea with unmeditated folk language and image, the greatest art had been created, the art of Homer and Shakespeare and of the cathedral of Chartres. To all this Joyce responded impatiently, 'You do not talk like a poet, you talk like a man of letters.'

There must have been pleasanter moments. Yeats invited Joyce to write a play after his own prescription for the theatre. Joyce agreed to do so, but in ten years' time—a five-year extension of the period he had specified to Russell. Yeats asked to keep his manuscripts, both poems and epiphanies; Joyce left them with him. These matters arranged, Joyce rose to go and delivered his parting shot: 'I am twenty. How old are you?' Yeats had turned thirty-seven three months before, but replied,

'Thirty-six,' realizing afterwards both his mistake and the reason for it. Joyce said with a sigh, as Yeats remembered, 'I thought as much. I have met you too late. You are too old.'

Joyce continued his attack on *Cathleen ni Houlihan* in *Ulysses*, where, however, his method changes from denunciation to parody. In Nighttown Old Gummy Granny thrusts a dagger towards Stephen's hand and says to him, 'Remove him, acushla. At 8.35 a.m. you will be in heaven and Ireland will be free. (*She prays.*) O good God, take him!' Yeats's Cathleen was equally highminded and bloodthirsty. While Joyce's attitude is not without occasional ambiguities, essentially the 'poor old woman' is admissible only as a comic fury.

Yeats, left alone with the poems and epiphanies, wrote to Joyce in the course of a four-page letter, 'You have a very delicate talent but I cannot yet say whether for prose or verse.' He saw the poems' thinness and the meagreness of the occasions which motivated them: 'Remember what Dr. Johnson said about somebody, "Let us wait until we find out whether he is a fountain or a cistern."' These chastening thoughts out of the way, he then declared that Joyce's technique was 'very much better than the technique of any young Dublin man I have met during my time. It might have been the work of a young man who had lived in an Oxford literary set.' Joyce sensed the acuteness of Yeats's remarks, for when he later gathered his poems together in the two collections, *Chamber Music* and *Pomes Penyeach*, he wished the titles to seem a little apologetic, as if he were half-resigning from the field of poetry even as he entered it.

Once he had received his degree, in October 1902, Joyce planned to endow his slow literary work with the speedy proceeds of a medical practice. On his way to the Ecole de Médecine in Paris, he entrusted his manuscripts for 'a motive' (as he told his brother) to George Russell. Presumably the reason was to keep himself in Russell's thoughts. Yeats, alerted by Lady Gregory as well as by Russell, met Joyce's train when it reached Euston Station at six o'clock the morning of 2 December 1902. He found Joyce 'unexpectedly amiable,' the young man 'did not knock at the gate with his old Ibsenite fury.' He took Joyce to see Arthur Symons and some editors, and encouraged him to offer poems to the magazines. From Paris Joyce sent 'All day I hear the noise of waters,' but Yeats judged it, because of a lack of subject, unsuitable for submission.

In Paris, Joyce tried to subsist on a job of reviewing books for the Dublin *Daily Express*, which Lady Gregory had secured for him. This was not without its vicissitudes, some of them of his own making. The editor, E. V. Longworth, sent him a new book of Lady Gregory, *Poets and Dreamers*, in the expectation of a favorable notice. It arrived in Paris at about the time that John Synge, at Lady Gregory's request, looked Joyce up there. Joyce treated both arrivals with the same severity. He complained in his review that the examples of folklore collected by Lady Gregory did not show the celebrated spontaneity and extravagance of the folk, but rather their senility, their want of imaginative plenitude. The folk plays at the end of her book he dismissed as 'dwarf-dramas.' This was the same term he applied to the play Synge showed him, *Riders to the Sea*, already praised by Yeats as 'Greek.' Applying the principles of Greek tragedy laid down by Aristotle, Joyce denounced the play from beginning to end. Synge paid absolutely no attention, the one attitude toward criticism by which Joyce could be impressed. Lady Gregory was less impervious. In *Ulysses* Buck Mulligan remonstrates with Stephen,

> —Longworth is awfully sick . . . after what you wrote about that old hake Gregory. O you inquisitional drunken jew jesuit! She gets you a job on the paper and then you go and

slate her drivel to Jaysus. Couldn't you do the Yeats touch?
He went on and down, mopping, chanting with waving graceful arms:
—The most beautiful book that has come out of our country in my time. One thinks of Homer.

Yeats had in fact so pronounced upon Lady Gregory's *Cuchalain of Muirthemne* a year before. It is part of Joyce's involuted and unresolvable feeling toward Yeats that such derogatory comments are invariably put in the mouths of other characters than the autobiographical Stephen.

In April 1903 Joyce had to come home because of his mother's illness. Yeats met him one day and asked about her condition. Joyce replied that she was still alive and it was uncertain whether she would die or not. Then he added, 'But these things really don't matter.' Yeats took the occasion to scold him for a quarrel with an English editor, and for other evidences of quarrelsomeness; he said afterwards that Joyce 'took it unexpectedly well.' It must have been at this chat that Joyce revealed how much he liked 'The Tables of the Law' and 'The Adoration of the Magi,' for when these were republished in 1904 Yeats referred to him, though not by name, in a prefatory note: 'I do not think I should have reprinted them had I not met a young man in Ireland the other day, who liked them very much and nothing else that I have written.'

Joyce mooned about Dublin for some months, then abruptly, in February 1904, began his first novel, *Stephen Hero*. By now he had given up, in part perhaps as a result of Yeats's lukewarm response, the idea of publishing his epiphanies as a separate book—Nathalie Sarraute's *Tropismes* is the kind of book he had conceived and abandoned. Instead he worked the epiphanies into his novel. With some qualms he also embarked on the process of modeling his hero on a legendary prototype, according Stephen the surname of Dedalus, as later he would relate

Bloom and Ulysses. This method, as T. S. Eliot was to note,* had been 'adumbrated' by Yeats, but Joyce adapted it daringly for prose. He also mocked his own method afterwards, in the poem 'The Holy Office,' by christening himself with a name more bathetic if scarcely less Greek, 'Katharsis-Purgative.' This poem gives flamboyant expression to Joyce's resentment of the literary establishment. Against their mystic ether he sings of crudity and straightforwardness. Yeats, a principal target, is represented, with deference to Dublin gossip, as

> him who hies him to appease
> His giddy dames' frivolities.

Joyce is eager to dissociate himself from the new Abbey Theatre, which had just received its patent:

> But I must not accounted be
> One of that mumming company,

lines which mock, rather wanly, 'To Ireland in the Coming Times,' where Yeats voiced his kinship with other Irish writers,

> Know that I would accounted be
> True brother of a company
> That sang, to sweeten Ireland's wrong,
> Ballad and story, rann and song. . . .

If the only contrary to fake spirituality is physicality, he is content to join that camp, scatological rather than airy:

> But all these men of whom I speak
> Make me the sewer of their clique.
> That they may dream their dreamy dreams
> I carry off their filthy streams. . . .

This abasement is only to exalt himself, at the end, as more lofty than they:

* See p. 92.

And though they spurn me from their door
My soul shall spurn them evermore.

The broadside was not immediately printed, perhaps for-
tunately, for when Joyce decided soon after to elope, he had to
turn for help to the very people he had just spurned evermore.
He wrote to Yeats offering him translations of two plays of
Hauptmann, *Before Sunrise* and *Michael Kramer*, both made
three years earlier. He mentioned also a pressing financial need.
Yeats returned the plays, saying that a friend (probably Lady
Gregory) had found Joyce's knowledge of German defective,
and that in any case the theatre must try to get the ear of the
public with Irish work. Though he had done his best to secure
writing assignments for Joyce, he could not send him money.

Furbished with small loans from other sources, Joyce and
Nora Barnacle left Dublin. His early writing on the Continent
falls into two phases, with an attack of rheumatic fever, that
lasted from July to September 1907, as the dividing line between
them. Following his illness he reconsidered the west of Ireland
in 'The Dead,' and he rewrote and renamed *Stephen Hero*. The
new version, *A Portrait of the Artist as a Young Man*, shows
greater confidence in his real powers, and more sense of what
he could not do. He overcame Yeats's influence on Stephen's
poem,

O, hold me still white arms, encircling arms!
And hide me, heavy hair,

by leaving it out. In Stephen's diary with which *A Portrait* ends,
Joyce has him quote from Yeats's *The Wind among the Reeds*
only to differ: 'Michael Robartes remembers forgotten beauty
and, when his arms wrap her round, he presses in his arms the
loveliness which has long faded from the world. Not this. Not
at all. I desire to press in my arms the loveliness which has not
yet come into the world.' Here Yeats is represented, not much

more fairly than in 'The Holy Office,' as static, emotionally
overfed, while Joyce commits himself to the sensations of the
world's cravings and of its inhabitants' hungers.

He had come to measure the Irish folk more justly. A sudden
shift is displayed in two versions of the same peasant which
appear in *Stephen Hero* and *A Portrait*. The first is ludicrous,
and might almost be mistaken for a passage out of a novel
by Charles Lever:

> One day an officer told a humorous story which was intended
> to poke fun at countrified ideas. . . .
> The story was this. The officer and a friend found them-
> selves one evening surprised by a heavy shower far out on the
> Killucan road and forced to take refuge in a peasant's cabin.
> An old man was seated at the side of the fire smoking a dirty
> cutty-pipe which he held upside down in the corner of his
> mouth. The old peasant invited his visitors to come near
> the fire as the evening was chilly and said he could not stand
> up to welcome them decently as he had the rheumatics. The
> officer's friend who was a learned young lady observed a figure
> scrawled in chalk over the fireplace and asked what it was.
> The peasant said:
> —Me grandson Johnny done that the time the circus was
> in the town. He seen the pictures on the walls and began
> pesterin' his mother for fourpence to see th' elephants. But
> sure when he got in 'an all divil elephant was in it. But it
> was him drew that there.
> The young lady laughed and the old man blinked his red
> eyes at the fire and went on smoking evenly and talking to
> himself:
> —I've heerd tell them elephants is most natural things,
> that they has the notions of a Christian . . . I wanse seen
> myself a picture of niggers riding on wan of 'em—aye and
> beating blazes out of 'im with a stick. Begorra ye'd have
> more trouble with the childre is in it now that [than] with
> one of thim big fellows.
> The young lady who was much amused began to tell the

peasant about the animals of prehistoric times. The old man
heard her out in silence and then said slowly:

—Aw, there must be terrible quare craythurs at the latther
ind of the world.

Stephen thought that the officer told this story very well
and he joined in the laugh that followed it.

Joyce had in mind the way that writers like Lever have succeeded, through the distancing haze of dialect, in rendering
the peasant clownish, just as he felt that Yeats and company
had used dialect to sentimentalize him. With considerable
courage, he displays Stephen along with the young lady and
the raconteur in a patronizing and imperceptive role. The city
visitors descend, in all their ermine, upon impoverishment,
emptiness, and disappointment. In the anecdote the circus described by the peasant sounds as forsaken as the bazaar in Joyce's
story 'Araby.' But in redoing the incident Joyce felt he had
something more to say about the old man, whom he kept for
Stephen's diary in *A Portrait*:

> John Alphonsus Mulrennan has just returned from the west
> of Ireland. (European and Asiatic papers please copy.) He
> told us he met an old man there in a mountain cabin. Old
> man had red eyes and short pipe. Old man spoke Irish.
> Mulrennan spoke Irish. Then old man and Mulrennan spoke
> English. Mulrennan spoke to him about universe and stars.
> Old man sat, listened, smoked, spat. Then said:
> —Ah, there must be terrible queer creatures at the latter
> end of the world.
> I fear him. I fear his redrimmed horny eyes. It is with him
> I must struggle all through this night till day come, till he
> or I lie dead, gripping him by the sinewy throat till . . . Till
> what? Till he yield to me? No. I mean him no harm.

Now the peasant is not seemingly stupid but obviously shrewd.
Joyce is amused by his Irish-speaking 'act' for tourists, and plays
upon the futility of the language revival. But the rest of the

conversation accords more identity to the peasant. His remark about creatures displays an indifferent eloquence. This is not the senile, driveling peasant Joyce had derided in reviewing *Poets and Dreamers*; rather it is an obstinate voice, unwilling to take the universe and the stars into its consciousnes, a kind of antitype to Stephen who as a schoolboy had represented himself as a point surrounded by the universe. This rejection is what rouses fear in Stephen, as if he recognized the old man to be an inimical force within himself as well as outside him. Whatever irony lies in a reference to 'the latter end of the world' when made in the latter end of Ireland is muted. Joyce has freed the peasant not only from dialect but from comic and romantic stereotypes.

As he reconstructed on the Continent his relationship with Ireland, he longed to assume his rightful position in Irish letters. The death of Synge early in 1909 seemed to open a vacancy, and Joyce returned to Dublin twice in that year. On one visit he stopped in London to see Yeats, and was received cordially in spite of 'The Holy Office.' In Dublin he was relieved to find that Yeats's Abbey Theatre, instead of yielding to the rabblement, was presenting a play of Shaw in defiance of the government censorship, and he wrote a friendly review for a Triestine newspaper. Perhaps feeling he had been too severe with Synge as well, he helped an Italian friend to translate *Riders to the Sea*, and later would arrange a production of the play in Zurich, with his wife in a minor role. This spirit of reconciliation was dampened in 1912 when at the last moment the Dublin publication of *Dubliners* was prevented.

In despair at this renewal of bad fortune, Joyce turned once more to Yeats, asking his intercession with an English publisher: 'You would do me a great service if you could intervene in its favour and, I hope, some service also to the literature of our country.' Yeats did not succeed in helping, but he did bring Joyce's work to the attention of Ezra Pound. One way that

Pound found to assist Joyce was to solicit grants in his behalf, and Yeats was always ready when called upon to write the principal recommendation. He was not given to unconsidered hyperboles, so that the letters in which he speaks of Joyce's 'fine talent,' and says, 'I believe him to be a man of genius,' were anything but routine. He took time to comment specifically on three of Joyce's books. Of *Chamber Music* he found it possible to say only that 'a little of it [was] very beautiful and all of it very perfect technically.' Understandably he liked one poem best, 'I hear an army,' for it resembled a little his own 'I hear the Shadowy Horses,' and was Joyce's only attempt in that collection at a complex symbolical theme. Of *Dubliners* Yeats said that it contained 'satiric stories of great subtlety,' and went on, 'There is not enough foreground, it is all atmosphere perhaps, but I look upon that as a sign of an original study of life.' In these stories he found the promise of 'a great novelist and a great novelist of a new kind.' Having read some parts of A *Portrait* in serial publication, he said they increased his conviction 'that he is the most remarkable new talent in Ireland today.' A little later he pronounced it 'a very great book.'

Yeats's enthusiasm was checked a little by Joyce's play *Exiles*, which both writers had hoped the Abbey Theatre might produce. Before reading it Yeats wrote to Pound, 'If it is at all possible the Abbey should face a riot for it.' But after reading it he informed Joyce that, while 'sincere and interesting,' it was not at all as good as A *Portrait*, and was 'too far from the folk drama' which the Abbey company could do best. He covered this rejection with compliments about Joyce's other work. He had heard about *Ulysses* from Pound, and looked forward to reading that.

This book began to appear in the *Little Review* in 1918, and when Yeats read the opening chapters, he praised them acutely, notwithstanding the many mocking references to himself. He wrote John Quinn in July,

> I am making a setting for my old age, a place to influence lawless youth, with its severity and antiquity. If I had had this tower when Joyce began I might have been of use, have got him to meet those who might have helped him. His new story in the *Little Review* looks like becoming the best work he has done. It is an entirely new thing—neither what the eye sees nor the ear hears, but what the rambling mind thinks and imagines from moment to moment. He has certainly surpassed in intensity any novelist of our time.

Although the separation of the mind from the senses may have troubled him, he was willing to give himself to the new mode. There is no record of his having read more of the book until he received his subscription copy in 1922, at about the time that he and his wife went to Paris and had dinner with the Joyces and the Pounds. On his return to Ireland, Yeats began *Ulysses* at once, and after some qualms commended it for qualities which he had observed in Joyce during their first meeting twenty years before. As he wrote Mrs. Olivia Shakespear in March, 'I am reading the new Joyce—I hate it when I dip here and there but when I read it in the right order I am much impressed. However I have but read some thirty pages in that order. It has our Irish cruelty and also our kind of strength and the Martello Tower pages are full of beauty. A cruel playful mind like a great soft tiger cat—I hear, as I read, the report of the rebel sergeant in '98: "O he was a fine fellow, a fine fellow. It was a pleasure to shoot him." ' Yeats was holding to his first image of the young man, whose acerbities age had greatly modified. Two months later Yeats was still at *Ulysses*, but now he read it and the Barsetshire novels alternately, Trollope as the aspirin for the headache of Joyce.

Late in 1922 Lady Gregory asked Joyce's permission to quote

in a book on the Irish literary movement a letter he had written
her in 1902. He refused brusquely to be quoted or even mentioned, since for twenty years there had been no public mention
of him or of his struggles or of his writings by anyone connected with the Irish literary movement. The only mild note in
his answer was a request to be remembered to Yeats. In part because of this exchange, Yeats some months later invited Joyce to
come and stay with him and his wife for a few days. 'If he
comes,' Yeats wrote a friend, 'I shall have to use the utmost in-
genuity to hide the fact that I have never finished *Ulysses*. I
shall have to hide him from the politicians, who are scarce ready
for his doctrine, while collecting what we have in the way of
men of letters.' Joyce, sensing a ceremonial and envisaging that
recognition might be almost as troublesome a stance in the
present as obscurity had been in the past, declined on the plea of
ill health. The invitation was renewed the following year and
again politely declined.

Like other people, Yeats devoted more time to thinking about
Ulysses than to reading it. He wished to assess its importance,
and in the first edition of *A Vision* (1926) he brilliantly related
it to the seemingly dissimilar writings of Pound, Eliot, and
Pirandello, as fragmenting an earlier unit of consciousness. In
them 'there is hatred of the abstract . . . the intellect turns upon
itself.' (Joyce's old refusal to allow Yeats his generalizations was
now turned round.) They 'either eliminate from metaphor the
poet's phantasy and substitute a strangeness discovered by historical or contemporary research or break up the logical proc-
esses of thought by flooding them with associated ideas or words
that seem to drift into the mind by chance; or set side by
side in *Henry IV*, *The Waste Land*, *Ulysses*—a lunatic among
his keepers, a man fishing behind a gas works, the vulgarity of a
single Dublin day prolonged through 700 pages—and delirium,
the Fisher King, Ulysses' wandering. It is as though myth and

fact, united until the exhaustion of the Renaissance, have now fallen so far apart that man understands for the first time the rigidity of fact, and calls up, by that very recognition, myth which now but gropes its way out of the mind's dark but will shortly pursue and terrify.' Yeats implies that in these writers myth, instead of merging with fact in a symbolic whole, has collided with it to produce a frenzied miscellany. This is a prelude to the manifestation of myth in some fearful, dehumanized form.

Joyce gives no evidence of having seen this edition of A Vision, of which only a few hundred copies were printed. It has been suggested that in Book II, Chapter II of *Finnegans Wake*, the diagram of Anna Livia Plurabelle parodies Yeats's intersecting cones, which in A Vision are emblems of conflicting opposites. If this were true, Yeats might seem to have played, as Joyce's straight man, a major part in the *Wake*. But whatever resemblance there may be, and there is not too much—one diagram is female and the other both male and female—is fortuitous. No verbal echoes of A Vision, such as would have been inevitable if Joyce had parodied the diagram, appear until after the first publication of Chapter II in 1928; those that do appear in a 1929 version derive from Yeats's poem 'Sailing to Byzantium' rather than from his book. Joyce must have come to know A Vision only in 1937, when the second edition appeared and he had Eugene Jolas read it aloud to him. According to Jolas, Joyce was deeply absorbed in 'the colossal conception,' and regretted that Yeats had not put it all into a creative work. As if to make good this deficiency, Joyce now inserted a multitude of Visionary allusions into the final version of his chapter.

The two books have other areas of affinity. Both writers attempted, like Joachim of Flora, to encompass history in a systematic formulation. They envisaged it as a four-part cycle, in Yeats symbolized by the four quarters of the moon, in Joyce by the four sections of his book. The relation of Anna Livia to the eternal masculine is not unlike that of the archetypal feminine to God in Yeats's early work. Humphrey Chimpden Earwicker as egg, and his sons Shem and Shaun as yolk and white, may also be compared to Yeats's conception of Unity of Being, in which various antitypes like Robartes and Aherne are the divided halves. What is involved here, however, is less influence than simultaneous perception. Where the two systems differ is in Joyce's rejection of life after death and of metaphysics in general, subjects made integral in Yeats's scheme.

While Yeats died before *Finnegans Wake* was published in its entirety, he read enough of one separately published section, *Anna Livia Plurabelle*, to comment on it in a late essay on Berkeley. He connected it with a tendency in modern literature toward distorted subjectivism: 'One thinks of Joyce's *Anna Livia Plurabelle*, Pound's *Cantos*, works of an heroic sincerity, the man, his active faculties in suspense, one finger beating time to a bell sounding and echoing in the depths of his own mind.' Much as he admired it, he could not sanction the suspension of the active faculties, which in *Ulysses* he had seen as the rejection of eye and ear. He had worried then over the 'rambling mind,' but now, made aware of the intensely lyrical qualities of Joyce's new work, he evolved for it the image of the sounding bell. Yet to concentrate so intently on the night mind was impossible for Yeats; to the end, even in his last poems where everything estimable is imperilled, he remained stubbornly loyal to the conscious mind's intelligible structure.

In their last years Yeats and Joyce found themselves often serving as each other's advocate. Yeats's reputation was secure in the English-speaking world, but had scarcely reached the Continent, where his submarine complexity defied translation. In Paris Joyce's friends, alive to the radical innovations in recent art, considered his passion for Yeats quaint, and they were startled also by his distaste for Eliot, his skepticism about Valéry and others. Joyce went on citing Yeats's poems and saying, 'No surrealist poet can equal that for imagination.' In June 1935 he wrote his son how at Fouquet's, pressed to quote something beautiful, he had recited Yeats for two hours. 'Everybody congratulated me on my extraordinary memory, my clear diction and my charming voice. Someone added: What a pity he is such a fool!'

On his side Yeats made a series of public statements. The first was on 9 August 1924, when he awarded the literary prizes at the Tailteann Games in Dublin. As a non-resident Joyce was ineligible, but Yeats, speaking for the other judges, George Russell and Lennox Robinson, as well as for himself, announced, 'We feel... that it is our duty to say that Mr. James Joyce's book, though as obscene as Rabelais, and therefore forbidden by law in England and the United States, is more indubitably a work of genius than any prose written by an Irishman since the death of Synge.' Three years later during a debate on copyright law, the piracy of *Ulysses* in the United States was mentioned, and Yeats replied to a question about it, 'I am not going to defend James Joyce. It is a very difficult question. Has the Senator ever looked into Rabelais? Rabelais is looked upon as one of the greatest masters of the past, and what is to be said of James Joyce may be said of Rabelais.... I do not know whether Joyce's *Ulysses* is a great work of literature. I have puzzled a good deal over that question.... All I will say is that it is the work of an heroic mind.' The invocation of Rabelais, a remote relative of Joyce at best, and of heroism, a quality not distinctively literary, showed Yeats combatting his own uneasiness.

He made a strong effort in 1932 to persuade Joyce to become a member of the Irish Academy, which with Bernard Shaw

Yeats was then founding. His words were gratifying: 'Of course the first name that seemed essential both to Shaw and myself was your own, indeed you might say of yourself as Dante said "If I stay who goes, if I go who stays?" Which means that if you go out of our list it is an empty sack indeed.' Joyce's response was well mannered, 'It is now thirty years since you first held out to me your helping hand.' But it had the firmness of a man who had lived long in exile and was unrelenting: 'I hope that the Academy of Irish Letters (if that is its title) which you are both forming will have the success it aims at. My case, however, being as it was and probably will be, I see no reason why my name should have arisen at all in connection with such an academy; and I feel quite clearly that I have no right whatsoever to nominate myself as a member of it. I am returning under separate cover the rules you were good enough to send me.' He made some amends by a respectful telegram to the poet on the occasion of his seventieth birthday in June 1935, though in later correspondence he learned to his distress that it had never been delivered. When Yeats died in 1939, Joyce sent a wreath and tribute to his grave. His own life was over in two more years.

Notwithstanding numerous melancholy qualifications, Yeats and Joyce had in common an intense desire to affirm human life. Blake, whose god was the Divine Humanity, was understandably a predecessor of both. For Yeats the method of literature was to raise the ordinary to the heroic, for Joyce a movement down was as required as a movement up, and he mingled ordinary, heroic, and mock-heroic without wishing to compound them. Yeats's mind generated, out of feelings of indignation and pain, images of perfection; Joyce said he preferred the footprint seen on the sand by Robinson Crusoe to the eternal city envisioned by John. The fallen world was his natural habitat. Yeats's impulse toward order makes the myths which appear in his work, such as the annunciation of a new era, ritualized, heraldic, supernatural; for Joyce similar myths appear unrehearsed, casual, part of the order of things. Yeats felt the need for sharp outlines, for a protrusive, exigent form; Joyce preferred to flesh out a more Gothic form with a multitude of particulars. He revels in the clutter by which Yeats, conceiving of art as purgation, was repelled. His manuscripts, at least the later ones, are revised by accretion, Yeats's by reduction. Their treatment of character offers a similar contrast: Yeats, in search of the frame of character, concerned himself a good deal with the dead, because their fundamental rhythms could be determined. Joyce, occupied with the vulgar accident, liked the conglomerate look of living material, and spent no time in memorials.

Their use of language reflects a difference in preconception. Yeats has no barrier about subjects, but in responding to unexalted occasions he guards a verbal formality. Even at his wildest, he maintains the poise, the authority of language. It is just this poise and authority which Joyce seems always to be disturbing, as if he were mounting a revolution against that worst of tyrannies, the lexical kind. Yeats is always attempting to further and to celebrate an aristocracy of culture, while Joyce, who depends more than Yeats upon such an aristocracy to read him, declines to endorse it, and in his work is concerned only with people who, he said, make less than a thousand pounds a year. His interests in the same way embraced parts of Dublin— slums and public houses—that Yeats found not so much vulgar as irrelevant, he being concerned with monuments or with houses that would some day have, if they had not already, the dignity of national shrines. Their conceptions of history have in common a cyclical theory, but Yeats makes many historical generalizations, and commits himself to a myth of decline which Eliot could share but which Joyce could not. For Joyce, whatever differences may exist between ages are not to be put in valuative terms. As he said of Stephen, all ages were as one to

<u>him,</u> resulting from the same laws of behavior, and equally remote from perfection. He did not for this reason condone the injustice against which Yeats raged, but he had no confidence in its regular rise and fall, only in its remaining discontinuous.

Between *voyeur* and *voyant* all literature must move, with the novelist inclined toward the first and the poet toward the second. Yet the sharpness of Joyce's perceptions comes from a conviction that all things are worth observing, which in turn derives from a sense of the self's freedom to observe them, while the vigor of Yeats's aspirations comes from an unwilling and yet acute acknowledgment of experience and of its shortcomings. In this middle ground their troubled friendship was possible.

IV

⇶ ⇷

Ez and Old Billyum

EZRA POUND, after attending the service for T. S. Eliot in Westminster Abbey in January 1965, memorialized an even older
association with W. B. Yeats by visiting the poet's widow in
Dublin. His friendship with Yeats began in 1908, six years before
he met Eliot. In a shrunken literary scene, it is tempting to try
to piece together the substance of this once drastic connection,
now diminished to history.

At the time of their first meeting in London, Pound was
twenty-three to Yeats's forty-three. He did not, like Joyce six
years earlier, find Yeats too old to be helped. Instead, he declared, with humility and yet some arrogance of his own, that
Yeats was the only poet worthy of serious study, and in later
years he recalled without chagrin having spent the years from
1908 to 1914 in 'learning how Yeats did it.' What he learned
was the 'inner form of the lyric or short poem containing an
image,' as in 'The Fish' ('Although you hide in the ebb and
flow / Of the pale tide when the moon is set'), and 'the inner
form of the line' (probably its rhythmical merger of 'dull, numb
words' with unexpected ones). Yeats offered further an example
of 'syntactical simplicity'; he had, for example, cut out inver-
sions and written with what Pound as late as 1914 considered

'prose directness,' in 'The Old Men Admiring Themselves in the Water': 'I heard the old, old men say, /"Everything alters." '

That Pound had already studied Yeats intently before coming to London is disclosed by the volume *A Lume Spento*, which he published in Venice on his roundabout way to England from Wabash College, and republished in 1965 with a new preface describing the poems as 'stale cream-puffs.' They are so, but show something anyway about the confectioner. The second poem, 'La Fraisne' (Old Provençal for ash tree), has a long 'note precedent' in Latin and Old Ezraic. Before explaining that the speaker in the poem is Miraut de Gazelas when driven mad by his love for Riels of Calidorn, Pound indicates that he wrote the poem in a mood like that of Yeats's *The Celtic Twilight*, a title which was intended to suggest a vague borderline between the physical and metaphysical worlds. He felt himself 'divided between a self corporal and a self ætherial,' or, as he defines it further, 'trans-sentient as a wood pool.' Such states, in which time is contained and transcended, possess Pound again, most notably in the descriptions of paradisal moods in the *Cantos*, but 'La Fraisne' itself does not offer this pitch of feeling. In the course of his self-exegesis, Miraut identifies himself with the ash tree; at one time he was a wise councillor, but now he has left 'the old ways of men' to lose himself in sylvan metamorphosis. He seems to follow the lead of two characters in Yeats's early poetry: Fergus, who abdicated to drive his brazen cars in the forest, and another royal abdicator, Goll, who belongs to the same dynasty as Arnold's 'Mycerinus.' Pound's line, 'Naught but the wind that flutters in the leaves,' echoes 'The Madness of King Goll,' where the refrain is: 'They will not hush, the leaves that round me flutter—the beech leaves old.' Miraut's thought that he is merging into the boles of ash wood owes something, like Pound's other early poem, 'The Tree,' to Yeats's poem, 'He Thinks of His Past Greatness

When a Part of the Constellations of Heaven': 'I have been a
hazel-tree and they hung / The Pilot Star and the Crooked
Plough / Among my leaves in times out of mind. . . .'

Other lines in 'La Fraisne,' where Miraut has 'put aside this
folly and the cold / That old age weareth for a cloak,' and
where he announces, 'For I know that the wailing and bitterness
are a folly,' echo words like 'wail' and 'folly' from the diction of
Yeats, and derive more particularly from his poem, 'In the Seven
Woods,' where the speaker has 'put away the unavailing out-
cries and the old bitterness / That empty the heart.' Blistered
in Provence, Miraut has been patched and peeled in Yeats's
first, third, and fourth volumes of verse, as well as in *The Celtic
Twilight*.

Yet the proximity to Yeats does not prevent 'La Fraisne' from
being identifiably Pound's configuration. Yeats portrays the madness of King Goll as a heroic state of mind superior to sanity,
while Councillor Miraut's mental condition is more equivocal,
even pathetic. Pound diverges also, after three stanzas, from the
formal regularity on which Yeats always insisted, so that he can
attempt to capture his hero's incoherence. In a passage, bold in
1908, he makes use of a series of broken sentences:

> Once when I was among the young men . . .
> And they said I was quite strong, among the young men,
> Once there was a woman. . .
> . . . but I forgot . . . she was. .
> . . . And I hope she will not come again.
>
> I do not remember. . . . .
>
> I think she hurt me once, but. .
> That was very long ago.

These are perhaps the most important dots in English poetry.
They show Pound already essaying what in *Mauberley* he calls

a 'consciousness disjunct.' In the later poem the pauses represent hesitations instead of panicky repressions:

> Drifted . . . drifted precipitate,
> Asking time to be rid of . . .
> Of his bewilderment; to designate
> His new found orchid. . . .

In the *Cantos*, like Eliot in *The Waste Land*, he usually leaves out dots, as if no one expected any longer the considerate guidance that prevailed in earlier poetry. But this mode begins in 'La Fraisne.'

If Pound translated Yeats, then, like one of his troubadours, sometimes literally and sometimes freely, Yeats responded to the change in atmosphere with which Pound surrounded his borrowings, and he did not dismiss him as an imitator. When he read *A Lume Spento*, with which Pound must have introduced himself, he called it 'charming,' an adjective Pound knew to be reserved. Still, Yeats could hardly have read the poem entitled 'Plotinus' without being tempted to rewrite it, syntactically and otherwise:

> As one that would draw thru the node of things
> Back sweeping to the vortex of the cone. . . .
>
> And then for utter loneliness, made I
> New thoughts as crescent images of *me*.

The vortexes are premonitory of Pound's later vorticist movement, but they also, with cones and crescents, anticipate metaphors of *A Vision*. Pound cannot be said to have put them into Yeats's head, for Yeats knew Plotinus well already, but he must have given them a new spin.

Yeats liked better Pound's book *Personae*, which appeared in April of the following year, 1909. The title proudly drew attention to the very point that had vexed William Carlos Williams in the first book, the assumption of a series of exotic roles.

For Pound, it was an attempt, by encompassing more situations and moods, to follow Walter Pater's advice and extend the self horizontally. Yeats's purpose in the seemingly similar doctrine of the mask, which he was then cultivating in early drafts of *The Player Queen*, and must have discussed with Pound, was a vertical deepening of the self by fusion with its opposite. For Yeats, Pound's theory, like Arthur Symons's version of Pater's impressionism, was too volatile and rootless, and suspiciously international. But, beyond the theory, he detected the young man's extraordinary talent; and Pound wrote elatedly to Williams, just after *Personae* was published, 'I have been praised by the greatest living poet.' This snub almost silenced Williams.

Yeats was in fact as pleased with his new friendship as Pound was. In December 1909, he wrote Lady Gregory that 'this queer creature Ezra Pound . . . has become really a great authority on the troubadours.' So much erudition of course amused him a little, too, and now or later he humorously accused Pound of trying to provide a portable substitute for the British Museum. He liked the way Pound devised to recite verse so that it sounded like music, with strongly marked time, yet remained intelligible, and he credited it with being a better method than that of Florence Farr, which a decade earlier he had so highly praised. But he noted also that Pound's voice was poor, sounding 'like something on a bad phonograph.' It may have been just the American accent emigrating to an Irish ear. Pound, for his part, thought Yeats's method of 'keening and chaunting with a *u*' absurd, and while he could effect no improvement, he obliged Yeats to admit, after half an hour's struggle, that poems such as those of Burns could not be wailed to the tune of *The Wind among the Reeds*. Each poet enjoyed condescending to the other.

Pound, as he began to flabbergast London with his passionate selections and rejections, found that his allegiance to Yeats was not shared by other writers whom he respected. The movement away from nineteenth-century poetry had begun. As John Butler Yeats wrote his son, 'The poets loved by Ezra Pound are tired of Beauty, since they have met it so often. . . . I am tired of Beauty my wife, says the poet, but here is that enchanting mistress Ugliness. With her I will live, and what a riot we shall have. Not a day shall pass without a fresh horror. Prometheus leaves his rock to cohabit with the Furies.' The vogue of ugliness was sometimes companioned by an insistence on man's limited and finite condition. T. E. Hulme was already in 1908, when he and Pound met, denouncing the romantic bog and leading the way to the classical uplands; by his rule, Yeats was wet and dim when he should have been dry and clear. On still other grounds T. S. Eliot, who battled Yeats for Pound's soul a few years later, declared Yeats an irrelevance in the modern world. By 1912 D. H. Lawrence, originally an admirer of Yeats, could say, 'He seems awfully queer stuff to me now—as if he wouldn't bear touching,' and he objected to Yeats's method of dealing with old symbols as 'sickly.' Another friend of Pound's, Ford Madox Ford, though not unreceptive to other monstrosities, informed Pound that Yeats was a 'gargoyle, a great poet but a gargoyle.'

Pound's determination to make it new combined with this voluble pressure to stint a little his admiration of Yeats as a model. Writing in *Poetry*, the then new Chicago review, in January 1913, he explained that Ford and Yeats were diametrically opposed because one was objective, the other subjective. While he grandly pronounced Yeats to be 'the only poet worthy of serious study,' he felt compelled to warn that the method of Yeats 'is, to my way of thinking, very dangerous.' The magistrate was severe: 'His art has not broadened much during the past decade. His gifts to English art are mostly negative; i.e., he has

stripped English poetry of many of its faults.' Yeats continued
to fall short. In 1913 Pound wrote Harriet Monroe that Ford
and Yeats were the two men in London, 'And Yeats is already
a sort of great dim figure with its associations set in the past.'
In the *Pisan Cantos* (LXXXII), the two men are weighed again,

> and for all that old Ford's conversation was better,
> consisting in *res non verba*,
> > despite William's anecdotes, in that Fordie
> > never dented an idea for a phrase's sake

> and had more humanitas

Such reservations did not prevent Pound from regarding Yeats
as a splendid bridge from Mallarmé and the symbolists, which
he could afford to cross on his way to founding imagism and
then vorticism. These movements, full of don'ts, extolled light,
clarity, and in general a Polaroid view of the verse line. Pound
knew, however, as Hulme, Lawrence, and Ford did not know,
that Yeats was still adaptable, and as eager to leave the '90s behind as they were. The books of verse he published in 1904 and
1910 reacted against his early manner, but he was still dissatisfied, and kept looking about for incitements for further change.
Pound was a perpetual incitement, mixing admiration with
remonstrance.

Another spur, now improbable, was Rabindranath Tagore,
whom Yeats met in June 1912. Tagore's poetry brought together,
Yeats felt, the metaphors and emotions of unlearned people
with those of the learned, coupling the fastidious with the
popular in the way that he had commended to Joyce ten years
before. Yeats remarked to Pound, unhinged by the same enthusiasm, that Tagore was 'someone greater than any of us—I
read these things and wonder why one should go on trying to
write.' Pointing to a description in Tagore's poem, 'The Banyan
Tree,' 'Two ducks swam by the weedy margin above their

shadows, and the child ... longed ... to float like those ducks among the weeds and shadows,' Yeats proclaimed, 'Those ducks are the ducks of real life and not out of literature.' His friend Sturge Moore was helping Tagore with the translation, and Yeats joined in the task, arguing with Moore about words. (He allowed Tagore to use the word 'maiden,' though in a later stage of dictional disinfection, when he was translating the *Upanishads* with another Indian, he insisted upon the word 'girl.') Soon he recognized that Tagore was 'unequal' and sometimes dull, but he saw mainly 'great beauty,' and wrote a fulsome introduction to *Gitanjali*.

Pound's own role in the modernization of Yeats began at first, like that of most mentors, uninvited. In October 1912 he persuaded Yeats to give *Poetry* a start with some new poems. Yeats sent them to Pound for transmittal, appending a note to ask that the punctuation be checked. The note was bound, as Pound said ruefully later, to 'create a certain atmosphere of drama.' He could not resist exceeding mere compliance by making three changes in Yeats's wording. In 'Fallen Majesty,' he impudently if reasonably deleted 'as it were' from the final line: 'Once walked a thing that seemed as it were a burning cloud.' In 'The Mountain Tomb,' he worried over the lines, 'Let there be no foot silent in the room, / Nor mouth with kissing or the wine unwet,' and altered 'or the' to 'nor with.' Then, with 'To a Child Dancing upon the Shore,'

> Being young you have not known
> The fool's triumph, nor yet
> Love lost as soon as won,
> Nor he, the best labourer, dead,
> And all the sheaves to bind,

Pound thought long and deep and then changed 'he' to 'him.'

At peace, he sent the poems to Harriet Monroe with the comment: 'I don't think this is precisely W. B. Y. at his best ... but

it shows a little of the new Yeats—as in the "Child Dancing."
"Fallen Majesty" is just where he was two years ago. "The
Realists" is also tending toward the new phase.' Pound, though
he had liked the hardness of 'No Second Troy,' was weary of
prolonging the celebrations of Maud Gonne as she had been
twenty years before. On the other hand, he welcomed the increasing directness that Yeats now usually aimed at. He conveyed something of these opinions to Yeats, and at the same
time duly informed him of the small changes he had made. To
his surprise, Yeats was indignant at this American brashness,
and Pound had to carry out mollification proceedings as recorded in his letters to Miss Monroe. For rhythm's sake Yeats
insisted upon restoring the spiritless 'as it were' to 'Fallen
Majesty,' though a year later he rewrote the line to get rid of
it. But Pound's other two revisions shook him. At first he modified the second passage to read, 'Nor mouth with kissing nor
the wine unwet,' but by the proof stage he recognized that
unwet wine would not do, and Pound's version, 'nor with wine
unwet,' appears in *Poetry*. In the third instance the battle of
the pronouns, he insisted upon 'he' rather than 'him,' but, made
aware of the grammatical sin, put a period after the third line
to replace the comma. On November 2, Pound transmitted
these partial restorations to Miss Monroe with the remark,
'Oh *la la*, ce que le roi désire!' Later the same day, he reported
a last change, eliminating 'Nor' before 'he':

> Final clinic in the groves of philosophy.

> Love lost as soon as won. (full stop)
> And he, the best labourer, dead

> peace reigns on parnassus.

Still enthralled by Tagore's verse, and still stung by Pound's
criticism, Yeats felt the challenge to his powers. It was probably

now that he confided to Pound, 'I have spent the whole of my
life trying to get rid of rhetoric. I have got rid of one kind of
rhetoric and have merely set up another.' For the first time in
years he asked for help, as his letters to Lady Gregory of 1 and 3
January 1913 make clear. In the former he writes: 'I have had
a fortnight of gloom over my work—I felt something wrong
with it. However on Monday night I got Sturge Moore in and
last night Ezra Pound and we went at it line by line and now
I know what is wrong and am in good spirits again. I am start-
ing the poem about the King of Tara and his wife ['The Two
Kings'] again, to get rid of Miltonic generalizations.' (Pound had
made 'Miltonic' a derogatory epithet.) He was later to redefine
what he and Pound had crossed out as 'conventional metaphors,'
presumably those turned abstract by overuse. In his second letter
to Lady Gregory he indicates that the whole experience has
given him diarrhea:

> My digestion has got rather queer again—a result I think
> of sitting up late with Ezra and Sturge Moore and some light
> wine while the talk ran. However the criticism I have got
> from them has given me new life and I have made that Tara
> poem a new thing and am writing with a new confidence
> having got Milton off my back. Ezra is the best critic of the
> two. He is full of the middle ages and helps me to get back
> to the definite and the concrete away from modern abstrac-
> tions. To talk over a poem with him is like getting you to
> put a sentence into dialect. All becomes clear and natural.
> Yet in his own work he is very uncertain, often very bad
> though very interesting sometimes. He spoils himself by too
> many experiments and has more sound principles than taste.

A letter which Pound sent Harriet Monroe summarizes the
sound principles if not the questionable taste he must have
communicated to Yeats. In terms ostentatiously graceless he
called for 'Objectivity and again objectivity, and expression;
no hind-side-beforeness, no straddled adjectives (as "addled

mosses dank"), no Tennysonianness of speech: *nothing* that you couldn't in some circumstance, in the stress of some emotion, *actually say*. Every *literaryism*, every book word, fritters away a scrap of the reader's patience, a scrap of his sense of your sincerity.' Though Yeats had been able to reconstruct much of his diction, he needed a jolt to complete the process. This Pound, by virtue of his downrightness, his good will, his unintimidatable character, his sense of himself as shocker, was peculiarly fitted to administer. For him, as for Auden later, poems were contraptions, and most of them were inefficient and needed overhaul. He had trained himself, like no one else, for the very task Yeats demanded of him. That Pound was able to give advice, and Yeats, notwithstanding age and fame, to take it and to admit having taken it, made their friendship, unlike many relations of literary men, felicitous.

The experience was, like most medicine, more than a little painful for Yeats; having requested Pound's help once, he had to submit to occasional further reproofs. He showed Pound 'The Two Kings' when it was finished, and Pound informed him (and said later in a review of *Responsibilities*) that it was like those *Idylls* written by a poet more monstrous even than Milton. Yeats wrote his father of this harsh verdict, and his father reassured him by saying that the poem had supremely what Tennyson never achieved—namely, concentration. Yeats took heart and believed that Pound this time was wrong. But he was nonetheless gratified when Pound, on reading the untitled last poem in *Responsibilities*, and especially the last lines—'till all my priceless things / Are but a post the passing dogs defile'— remarked that Yeats had at last become a modern poet. An image of urination had finally brought Pound to his knees.

Yeats, while acknowledging Pound's critical penetration and quite liking him as a person, was perplexed about his poetry.

He quarreled with the rhythms of its free verse as 'devil's metres.' Many of the poems did not seem to Yeats fully achieved. When in 1913 Harriet Monroe offered him a prize for 'The Grey Rock,' Yeats urged her to give it to Pound instead; he said candidly, 'I suggest him to you because, although I do not really like with my whole soul the metrical experiments he has made for you, I think those experiments show a vigorous creative mind. He is certainly a creative personality of some sort, though it is too soon yet to say of what sort. His experiments are perhaps errors, I am not certain; but I would always sooner give the laurel to vigorous errors than to any orthodoxy not inspired.' Although Pound's work was not to Yeats's taste any more than Joyce's, he could not fail to sense that here, too, was a kind of alien talent. The following year he spoke at a *Poetry* dinner in Chicago, and said again of Pound, 'Much of his work is experimental; his work will come slowly; he will make many an experiment before he comes into his own.' But he read two poems which he judged of 'permanent value,' 'The Ballad of the Goodly Fere' and 'The Return.' The latter he complimented, in that slightly histrionic rhythm for which Joyce mocked him in *Ulysses*,* as 'the most beautiful poem that has been written in the free form, one of the few in which I find real organic rhythm.' He quoted it again later in *A Vision*, where it jibed with his theory of cyclical repetition. He was consciously, doggedly allowing virtue in Pound's work, though he had no wish to enroll in the new school which his former pupil had opened. On many matters they continued to dispute, and Pound summarized almost with satisfaction the quarrelsomeness of a meeting the next year: 'The antipodes of our two characters and beliefs being in more vigorous saliency.'

During the winter of 1913-14, and the two following winters,

* See above, p. 42.

Yeats wished to be away from London with a secretary who
could do some typing and also read to him Doughty's poems
and (anticipating Auden) Icelandic sagas. He had formed the
plan with Pound as companion in mind, and Pound with misgivings agreed to put himself out for the sake of English letters.
He expected that Yeats would sometimes amuse him but often,
because the occult was so irresistible a subject, bore him. To
his partial surprise, life with Yeats in a four-room Sussex cottage
proved contented and placid. He wrote Williams that Yeats
was 'much finer *intime* than seen spasmodically in the midst
of the whirl.' With more polish he described life at Stone
Cottage nostalgically in Canto LXXXIII:

> There is fatigue deep as the grave.
> The Kakemono grows in flat land out of mist
>   sun rises lop-sided over the mountain
>   so that I recalled the noise in the chimney
> as it were the wind in the chimney
>   but was in reality Uncle William
> downstairs composing
> that had made a great Peeeeacock
>   in the proide ov his oiye
>   had made a great peeeeeeecock in the . . .
> made a great peacock
>   in the proide of his oyyee
>
> proide ov his oy-ee
> as indeed he had, and perdurable
>
> a great peacock aere perennius
>   or as in the advice to the young man to
> breed and get married (or not)
>   as you choose to regard it
>
> at Stone Cottage in Sussex by the waste moor
> (or whatever) and the holly bush
>   who would not eat ham for dinner

because peasants eat ham for dinner
   despite the excellent quality
and the pleasure of having it hot

well those days are gone forever
   and the travelling rug with the coon-skin tabs
and his hearing nearly all Wordsworth
   for the sake of his conscience but
preferring Ennemosor on Witches

did we ever get to the end of Doughty:
   The Dawn in Britain?
      perhaps not

While Yeats's aristocratic pride and his reaching over Words-worth for witches amused Pound still, he recognized that these two foibles received a kind of immortal warranty by their reflection in 'The Peacock' and 'The Witch.'

At Stone Cottage, Pound taught Yeats after a fashion to fence, while Yeats offered reciprocal lessons, as dreaded, in spiritualism and related subjects. These proved, however, more apposite to his own interests than Pound had anticipated. For when Yeats was writing essays for Lady Gregory's *Visions and Beliefs in the West of Ireland,* setting them in the context of the *tradition à rebours,* Pound was devoting himself to editing Ernest Fenollosa's translations of the Noh plays of Japan. These were just as crowded with ghosts and other extraterrestrial creatures. East and West met in the astral envelope as well as in Connemara. In the edition he now made of the Noh plays, Pound refers frequently to parallels furnished him by Yeats, and speaks with unwonted respect of such matters as 'the "new" doctrine of the suggestibility or hypnotizeability of ghosts,' though he preserves his dignity by an alibi: only the merit of the Japanese poetry has brought him to this pass. Pound's versions

of Noh convene a kind of grand international festival with
entries from India, Japan, England, the United States, and
Ireland. The Samurai are particularly at home in Kiltartan or
Aran:

> I've a sad heart to see you looking up to Buddha, you who
> left me alone, I diving in the black rivers of hell. Will soft
> prayers be a comfort to you in your quiet heaven, you who
> knew that I'm alone in that wild, desolate place?

> Times out of mind am I here setting up this bright branch,
> this silky wood with the charms painted on it as fine as the
> web you'd get in the grass-cloth of Shinobu, that they'd be
> still selling you in this mountain.

> I had my own rain of tears; that was the dark night, surely.

The Noh plays were more to Yeats's taste than to Pound's:
by 1918 Pound was prematurely dismissing them as a failure.
He linked them in this disgrace with Yeats's long essay, *Per
Amica Silentia Lunae*, which with its hypothesis of antiselves
and daimons must still have seemed too occult for the mint
assayer's son. Whether he also dismissed the prefatory poem to
this work, 'Ego Dominus Tuus,' is not clear, though his allusion to it as a dialogue of 'Hic' and 'Willie' (for 'Ille') perhaps
implies some dissatisfaction, beyond his unwillingness to resist
polylingual jokes. He was prepared to believe again, as he said
in 1920, that Yeats was 'faded.'

Yeats had entered a period of much greater assurance. The
Noh plays, so fortuitously put in his hands, had won without
his being aware of it the battle with naturalistic drama which he
had himself been fighting in beleaguered fashion. Here was the
authorization he needed for leaving probability in the lurch,
by abolishing scenery so the imagination would be untrammeled,
by covering faces with masks, by portraying character in broad

strokes—emptied of Ibsen's convincing details—through isolat-
ing the moment in which some irrevocable deed separates a man
from his fellows as well as from his own idiosyncrasies. He was
also prompted to new and more reckless devices, the symbolic
dance as a climax to suggest the impingement of the timeless
upon the actual, the preternatural shudder from the sudden
lighting-up of a ruined place, the assumption of someone else's
human form by a spirit or god. Yeats saw how he might focus
an entire play, as he had entire poems, on a single metaphor.
That the Noh plays were often blurred in effect did not ruffle
him; the form, he saw, could be improved. He kept the strangeness and increased the dramatic tension, splicing natural with
preternatural in order, unpredictably, to heighten the human
dilemma. The Yeatsian paradox was to explode verisimilitude
by miracle for the purposes of a more ultimate realism.

The result was the first of his plays for dancers, *At the Hawk's
Well*, and to some degree almost all his subsequent plays. Hap-
pily, Ezra Pound proved to have an aptitude for the criticism of
drama as well. He offered many suggestions about scenery and
timing; he found the indispensable Japanese dancer Michio Itō;
and he helped Yeats to clarify the play. For a time, it seemed
that his dramatic ability might receive professional sanction. He
wrote a skit which Yeats encouraged him to enlarge, thinking it
might be suitable for presentation at the Abbey Theatre, but
it was adjudged, by the then manager, too full of indecencies.
Then Yeats recommended to Lady Gregory that Pound fill in as
manager of the Abbey for a four-month period, but this plan
also was vetoed. Surviving these rebuffs, Pound remained indispensable; he observed Yeats locked in struggle with a long-
unfinished tragedy, and irreverently proposed it be made a comedy instead. The firecracker went off, Yeats was exhilarated, and
The Player Queen reached completion. Both Pound's moral

impudence about experience and Yeats's theme in the play—
the necessity of lying—would have pleased Wilde.

In the midst of vorticism and daimonism both poets were
distracted toward marriage. Yeats had trouble unmaking the
fealty to Maud Gonne as symbol, if not as woman, which he
had so often declared. He wrote a poem, 'His Phoenix' (which
Pound dismissed as 'a little bad Yeats') to contrast her more
gaily than usual with the current lot of women, 'There's Margaret and Marjorie and Dorothy and Nan, / A Daphne and a
Mary who live in privacy,' with the defiant conclusion, 'I knew
a Phoenix in my youth, so let them have their day.' He was
indulging here a private joke by making a list of Pound's girl   LOL
friends. Among them Dorothy was pre-eminent. This was
Dorothy Shakespear, with whose mother, Olivia, Yeats had
been in love during the 'nineties. Pound married Dorothy in
April 1914. Then Yeats, after the Easter Rebellion had widowed
Maud Gonne, felt duty bound to offer her marriage, though he
hesitated to bed an obsessive conviction. (Pound saw her in
the same way: when he wished to characterize Yeats's occult
interests, just as when Yeats wished to characterize Pound's
political ideas, each compared the other to Maud Gonne.) Her
refusal was a relief. The next year Yeats married Georgie Hyde-
Lees, a cousin and close friend of Pound's wife, and Pound
served as best man. The two poets met often after their mar-
riages. After Pound went to the Continent in 1920, they met in
Paris in 1922, in Sicily in 1925, in Rapallo in 1928, 1929-30,
1934, and in London in 1938. Yet, as so often, separate house-
holds made for a subtle disconnection of friendship.

Pound's work had become more ambitious. After *Lustra*, he
wrote *Propertius, Mauberley,* and the first *Cantos.* Yeats dis-
concerted him in 1916 by saying that Pound's new work gave
him 'no asylum for his affections.' Pound wrote the criticism to

Kate Buss, but cautioned her about repeating it. Perhaps in part because he recognized some justice in it, Pound moved away from purely satirical poems like many in *Lustra,* and in the *Cantos* (LXXXI) he subscribes fully to Yeats's principle:

> What thou lovest well remains,
> the rest is dross
> What thou lov'st well shall not be reft from thee
> What thou lov'st well is thy true heritage

It is hard to discover Yeats's views of Pound's new works. He told Pound in 1920 that he liked *Mauberley,* and he tried to suspend judgment about the *Cantos.*

His attitude toward Pound between 1915 and 1925 can however be elicited from *A Vision,* the book he began in October 1917 just after his marriage. In the charactcrology which formed a large part of this book, Yeats classified contemporaries and men of the past in terms of phases of the moon. Pound was slowly becoming an abstraction, something analyzed at a distance. The early drafts, written between 1918 and 1922, placed Pound with Nietzsche as denizen of the twelfth lunar phase, called the phase of the Forerunner. He is Forerunner to men of fuller consciousness including, with chronological indifference, Yeats himself. But when the book was published in 1926, Pound's name was omitted; Yeats probably feared to give pain. Though Phase 12 was not a bad perch, Pound occupied it in a disharmonious way. The Phase-12 man who is 'in phase' follows Zarathustra's exhortation by heroically overcoming himself. (Yeats speaks elsewhere of Pound's effort at total self-possession, but does not seem to have regarded it as successful.) He is thereby enabled to assume his true mask which is lonely, cold, and proud, and to formulate a subjective philosophy that exalts the self in the presence of its object of desire. While Yeats may have thought of imagism as offering an esthetic philosophy of this kind, he had primarily in mind Nietzsche's projection of a superior world. In phase, the Phase-12 mind is a jetting fountain of personal life, of noble extravagance. It loathes abstraction as much as Pound did, and everything it considers comes clothed in sound and metaphor.

But if the man of this phase is 'out of phase,' the result is much less satisfactory. Unable to discover his true mask, he assumes almost in frenzy a series of self-conscious poses. Here Yeats must have thought of Pound's *Personae*, and perhaps of Pound's own Bergsonian statement in *Gaudier-Brzeska*: 'One says "I am" this, that, or the other, and with the words scarcely uttered one ceases to be that thing. I began this search for the real in a book called *Personae*, casting off, as it were, complete masks of the self in each poem. I continued in long series of translations, which were but more elaborate masks.' Always in reaction, yet according to Yeats always hesitant, the out-of-phase man becomes a prey to facts, which drug or intoxicate him. More by chance than choice, he turns to a false mask, which offers instead of splendid loneliness the isolation of some small protesting sect; and he defends this role by 'some kind of superficial intellectual action, the pamphlet, the violent speech, the sword of the swashbuckler.' He oscillates between asserting some pose or, if preoccupied with outward things, asserting a dogmatism about events which depends too much upon the circumstances that produced it to have lasting value. Yeats is thinking here of Pound's adherence to Major Douglas's theories of social credit.

Even if Yeats penciled Pound into Phase 12, he could not fail to think of him also for Phase 23, which is the phase of our age and of its dominant art. Ultimately, he decided to transfer Pound completely to this later and less desirable phase; he saw him as neither arch-individualist nor forerunner but as a dissolving mind, subject to losses of self-control. What immediately impelled this unhappy demotion was the sight of Pound feeding all the stray cats in Rapallo in 1928. This undifferentiated pity, pity 'like that of a drunken man,' was quickly connected by Yeats to the hysterical pity for general humanity left over from the romantic movement. He had observed and blamed it in other writers, notably Sean O'Casey and Wilfred Owen. All three now seemed to belong to Phase 23, the theme of which is Creation through Pity.

The man of Phase 23 studies the external world for its own sake, and denies every thought that would make order of it. Instead of allowing the fountain of the mind to overflow, as in Phase 12, he lets the cauldron of the world boil over. Not only is causation denied, as Pound once remarked to Yeats, only sequence being knowable, but even sequence is destroyed. Yeats returned to this idea of A Vision in other essays, where he complained of the Cantos specifically: 'There is no transmission through time, we pass without comment from ancient Greece to modern England, from modern England to medieval China; the symphony, the pattern, is timeless, flux eternal and without movement.' In subsequent art, violations like Pound's have ceased to appear violative, but Yeats was not yet accustomed to them. He found an Eastern parallel for such work not in Pound's favorite Easterner, Confucius (who to Yeats seemed an eighteenth-century moralist, pulpited and bewigged), but in Sankara, the ninth-century founder of a school of Vedantism which conceives of mental and physical objects as 'alike material, a deluge of experience breaking over us and within us, melting limits whether of line or tint; man no hard bright mirror dawdling by the dry sticks of a hedge, but a swimmer, or rather the waves themselves.' The new literature of the Cantos, of Virginia Woolf's novels, melted limits of plot, of logic, of character, of nationality, of authorship. In a letter, Yeats complained that Pound and his school prided themselves on what their poems did *not* contain, all that might stop the flood, the conscious mind's capacity for intelligibleness and form.

Remembering his old view that Pound was too preoccupied with experiment, Yeats in *A Vision* asserts that in Phase 23 everything is seen from the point of view of technique and is investigated technically rather than imaginatively. Technical mastery offers the man of his phase his only refuge from masterless anarchy. Denying its subjective life, the mind delights only in the varied scene outside the window, and asks to construct a whole which is all event, all picture. Because of this submission to outwardness, the man of Phase 23 wishes to live in his exact moment of time as a matter of conscience, and, says Yeats, defends that moment like a theologian. He has in mind here Pound's imagist predilection, as well as his forever and dogmatically 'making it new.'

Yeats noticed also that men of this phase, not only Pound but Joyce and Eliot, were apt to contrast some present scene with a mythical one.* By holding apart what should be joined, the Phase-23 mind heralds further loss and eventual extinction of personality, and a world in which rights are swallowed up in duties and force is adored so that society turns into a mechanism. At variance with some of his later prose, Yeats explicitly deplores here an inevitable alliance of this phase and its succeeding phases with a regimented state.

After the first edition of *A Vision* was published early in 1926, Yeats grew dissatisfied with some of it, included the pretense that it was translated from an Arabic manuscript. In 1928 he came to Rapallo intending to work on it some more. He showed Pound a poem he had translated 'From the *Antigone*,'

* See pp. 50-51.

and was again convinced of his neighbor's critical acumen. After
looking over what 'the Yeats' (as Pound jocularly called him)
had written,

> Overcome, O bitter sweetness,
> The rich man and his affairs,
> The fat flocks and the fields' fatness,
> Mariners, wild harvesters;
> Overcome God upon Parnassus;
> Overcome the Empyrean; hurl
> Heaven and Earth out of their places—
> *Inhabitant of the soft cheek of a girl*—
> *And into* the same calamity,
> *That* brother and brother, friend and friend,
> Family and family,
> City and city may contend
> By that great glory driven wild—
> Pray I will and sing I must
> And yet I weep—Oedipus' child
> Descends into the loveless dust.

Pound saw that the eighth line must become the second; he
changed 'And into' to 'That in,' and dropped 'That' before
'brother.' Yeats accepted the corrections. They may have given
him an idea, which was half a jest, of complimenting Pound by
prefacing A Vision with a series of papers under the common
title, 'A Packet for Ezra Pound.' The irony of this tribute was
that of all Yeats's books A Vision, with its detailed scheme of
life and the afterlife, was most antipathetic to Pound's conception of art as liberated from deliberate rule or abstract theory.
So 'A Packet' would pit Yeats against his surest castigator.

Acting on this impulse, Yeats began the 'Packet' with a description of Rapallo and then a discussion of the poet 'whose
art is the opposite of mine.' He summarized a conversation he
had had with Pound about the *Cantos,* and explained the poem

enough (as he wrote a friend) to keep Pound neighborly. He did his best, in fact, to present sympathetically Pound's mode of marshaling in spurts certain increasingly enforced themes, though he admitted being unable to overcome his feeling that the *Cantos* were fragmentary, that in them conventions of the intellect were abolished to satisfy an illusion that what is primal is formless, and that discontinuity had become a shibboleth.

Yeats also included in 'A Packet' a letter to Pound warning the expatriate against accepting public office: 'Do not be elected to the Senate of your country. I think myself, after six years, well out of mine. Neither you nor I, nor any other of our excitable profession, can match those old lawyers, old bankers, old business men, who, because all habit and memory, have begun to govern the world. They lean over the chair in front and talk as if to half a dozen of their kind at some board-meeting, and, whether they carry their point or not, retain moral ascendancy.' Pound, deep in correspondence with several senators, was not at all convinced. In Canto LXXX he responded, 'If a man don't occasionally sit in a senate / how can he pierce the darrk mind of a / senator?' As for the bankers, Pound's special detestation, he devoted his pasquinade, 'Alf's Eighth Bit,' in the *New English Weekly* (1934) to reforming Yeats's view of them:

> Vex not thou the banker's mind
>   (His *what?*) with a show of sense,
> Vex it not, Willie, his mind,
>   Or pierce its pretence
> On the supposition that it ever
> Was other, or that this cheerful giver
> Will give, save to the blind.

The only other part of *A Vision* on which Pound commented directly was not from 'A Packet' but from the ending. Yeats

wrote there: 'Day after day I have sat in my chair turning
a symbol over in my mind, exploring all its details, defining and
again defining its elements, testing my convictions and those
of others by its unity, attempting to substitute particulars for
an abstraction like that of algebra ... Then I draw myself up
into the symbol and it seems as if I should know all if I could
but banish such memories and find everything in the symbol.'
From Pound's point of view, symbols interfered with experience
instead of letting experience coalesce into its natural pattern.
In Canto LXXXIII he alluded to Yeats's perorative remarks,
and connected them with 'Sailing to Byzantium' (a poem
Pound had published in *The Exile* in 1928), where Yeats had
asked to be gathered into 'the artifice of eternity.' Contrary to
Yeats, Pound insisted,

> Le Paradis n'est pas artificiel
> And Uncle William dawdling around Notre Dame
> in search of whatever
>   paused to admire the symbol
> with Notre Dame standing inside it
> Whereas in St Etienne
>   or why not Dei Miracoli:
> mermaids, that carving,

Pound differs with Yeats on architecture as on paradise; he
ironically suggests that Mary's presence is diminished rather
than enhanced by the symbolic portentousness of her cathedral.
He subtly compares her to Yeats ingested into his own cathe-
dral-like *Vision*. As churches, Pound prefers less solipsistic structures like St. Etienne in Périgueux or Pietro Lombardo's Santa
Maria dei Miracoli in Venice, and he repeats his earlier praise
of Tullio Lombardo's carvings of sirens or mermaids on the
latter church. As literature, Pound prefers to *A Vision* those
poems of Yeats where there is less sense of the writer's being

cocooned. His mild example is 'Down by the Salley Gardens,' from which he slightly misquotes a few lines later:

> the sage
> delighteth in water
> the humane man has amity with the hills
>
> as the grass grows by the weirs
> thought Uncle William. . . .

Yeats did not live to read the mixed blame and praise meted out to him in the *Pisan Cantos*, but he had another occasion to sample Pound's opinion of him. At the age of sixty-nine he wondered if he might not be too old for poetry. Fearing to outwrite his talent, he went to Rapallo in June 1934 primarily to show Pound a new play, *The King of the Great Clock Tower*. Pound was hard to divert from politics; he took the play, however, and next day rendered his verdict, 'Putrid!' In recounting this experience, Yeats allowed it to be thought that this was all Pound said, and that it was a sign, like his violent political *parti pris*, of a mind too exacerbated to be reliable. But in an unpublished journal he does Pound more justice. What Pound told him was that the lyrics of the play were written in 'Nobody language' and would not do for drama. Far from defying this judgment, Yeats was humbled by Pound's criticism of his diction, willing as always to undergo any indignity for the work's sake. In his notebook he wrote, 'At first I took his condemnation as the confirmation of my fear that I am now too old. I have written little verse for three years. But "nobody language" is something I can remedy. I must write in verse, but first in prose to get structure.' He liked the new songs well enough to publish the play with a preface which, without mentioning Pound by name, wryly repeated his verdict. At the same time, as if to guard against any possibility that Pound's criticism might still apply even after revision, Yeats wrote another play on the same theme, A *Full Moon in March*, where the songs of the head (which is lopped off in both plays) are more concrete. He also let Pound know, through Olivia Shakespear, that *The King of the Great Clock Tower* had been his most successful play at the Abbey.

Pound was not abashed; he had reverted to the pejorative view of Yeats's work as 'dim' or 'faded' that he had taken from time to time in the past, and he wrote Basil Bunting in 1936 that Yeats was 'dead,' 'clinging to the habit of being a writer,' that the recent poetry was 'slop.' In another letter to Bunting he found 'increasing difficulty' in 'reading the buzzard.' For Pound, Yeats, in spite of devoted ministrations, had come alive only for brief intervals. But at the last meeting of the two poets, which took place late in 1938 in London, Pound said he liked very much some of Yeats's recent poems, and Yeats, accustomed to Pound's impertinent rebuff, was proportionately disarmed by his praise. Pound's most recent testimonial of quizzical admiration for Yeats is a parodic version of 'Under Ben Bulben' written in a Wabash version of Irish dialect, which he first published in 1958:

> Neath Ben Bulben's buttocks lies
> Bill Yeats, a poet twoice the soize
> Of William Shakespear, as they say
>
> Down Ballykillywuchlin way.
>
> Let saxon roiders break their bones
> Huntin' the fox
> thru dese gravestones.

Yeats in his last years made a fresh effort to formulate his view of Pound without recourse, this time, to the symbology of *A Vision*. He was compiling his *Oxford Book of Modern Verse*, and the preface provided a good occasion to fence with his old fencing-master. As he thought about Pound and selected three of his poems ('The River-Merchant's Wife: A Letter,' a passage from *Propertius*, and Canto XVII), Yeats remarked to Dorothy Wellesley that Pound's work conveyed 'a single strained attitude,' that Pound was 'the sexless American professor for all his violence.' In the preface he said more discreetly: 'When I consider his work as a whole I find more style than form; at moments more style, more deliberate nobility and the means to convey it than in any contemporary poet known to me, but it is constantly interrupted, broken, twisted into nothing by its direct opposite, nervous obsession, nightmare, stammering confusion.' The trait of nobility mentioned by Yeats was one that Pound had lauded in reviewing *Responsibilities* in 1916; returning the compliment, Yeats prefixed the word 'deliberate' to indicate how a consciously assumed role might flag at moments into total disorder. Not having achieved personal unity, Pound, in Yeats's view, had failed in his effort to get all the wine into the bowl. Pound did not respond directly, though in the *Cantos* he remarks briefly, but twice, that Yeats, like Possum (Eliot) and Lewis, and unlike Orage, 'had no ground to stand on.' Orage stood on the firm ground of Major Douglas's economics.

While not retreating from his innovations, Pound has often owned the tentativeness of the method he adopted for the *Cantos*. When in 1917 he published in *Poetry* the first versions of Cantos I, II, and III, he was almost apologetic in contrasting their broken form with Browning's: 'You had one whole man? / And I have many fragments.' At the same time, 'the modern world / Needs such a rag-bag to stuff all its thoughts in.' After having read and helped revise *The Waste Land*, he wrote Eliot sadly in 1921, 'I am wracked by the seven jealousies, and cogitating an excuse for always exuding my deformative secretions in my own stuff, and never getting an outline.' This same humility prompted him until 1937 to treat the published *Cantos* as only 'drafts,' and they became final just by passage of time, not change of heart. In his most recent writing, he returns, as in Canto 116, to his old sense of brave yet possibly unrealized effort:

> but the beauty is not in the madness
> Tho my errors and wrecks lie about me.
> and I cannot make it cohere.

Pound has, in fact, always recognized some force in Yeats's objections.

For his part, Yeats did not summarily dismiss what Pound was attempting. The Japanese professor Shotaro Oshima went to visit him in the summer of 1938, and expressed dissatisfaction with the poems collected in Pound's *Active Anthology*. Yeats replied, 'Even those pieces composed by ellipsis have a triumphant combination of the visual and the imaginative.' He had come to identify Pound with ellipsis. In some of his later poems he endeavors to make room for a comparable if not identical agitation, by incorporating in them a direct challenge to the symmetry of the universe. He produces disruption by a refrain that embodies most of the hesitations, denials, and unspoken thoughts which Pound conveyed by ellipsis or discontinuity. So in 'What Then?' the ghost of Plato is summoned to question in the refrain everything that has been affirmed in the body of the stanza:

> 'The work is done,' grown old he thought,
> 'According to my boyish plan;
> Let the fools rage, I swerved in naught,
> Something to perfection brought';
> *But louder sang that ghost, 'What then?'*

With such devices Yeats, who had generally conceived of reality under the figure of a sphere, acknowledges another force, which might be called the *anti-sphere*—a contemptuous, unassimilable

force which mocks our enterprise. Plato's ghost is a more repu-
table symbol for anarchy than Pound would have used, but in
its lofty way it counters any hope of accommodation, any content with established forms. Perhaps Pound's liking for Yeats's
last poems came from understanding that they were not un-
concessive, that they too acknowledged the domain of incoherence.

The relationship of the two men had long ceased to be that
of master and disciple. Though Pound referred to Yeats as
'Uncle William' or 'Old Billyum,' it was he who after 1912 often
assumed the avuncular role. As a matter of fact, they be-uncled
each other. The sense that Yeats could profit from his corrections must have reinforced Pound's sense of his own independent
talent. To have kept Yeats up to the mark was a heady accom-
plishment. But Pound went his own way and, notwithstanding
his penchant for quoting, and lecturing, Yeats in the *Cantos*,
their later work is quite dissimilar. The principal and determin-
ing divergence between them remains their conceptions of form,
which for Yeats is usually an hourglass, mined until it turns
over, while for the later Pound, insofar as it can be characterized
at all (and both he and his critics have had difficulty), it is an
impromptu breakthrough, not to be prepared in advance or
enshrined in retrospect. Yeats was eager to offset Pound's
world, one of seeming flow but actually, as he insisted to Stephen
Spender, static and tapestrylike, with his own, which brought
solids to the melting-point.

The two poets were equally engrossed in what Pound calls
'top flights of the mind,' moments often signaled in him by a
pool of water, in Yeats by a sense of being blessèd or birdlike or
of shaking all over. Their metaphysics are not the same, however, for Pound at least on some occasions insists upon the
power of the objective, external image to compel or lure the
mind to recognize it, as if he found Yeats too arbitrary in his

constructions, while at other times he declares, 'UBI AMOR IBI
OCULUS EST,' or as he says elsewhere,

> nothing matters but the quality
> of the affection—
> in the end—that has carved the trace in the mind
> dove sta memoria. . . .

The two positions were dovetailed by Pound's insistence that
the writer needs above all 'continuous curiosity,' to insure that
enough life will be 'vouchsafed' for him to work with; but
curiosity and observation are, as he reiterates in the *Cantos*,
only a start, the vital ingredient being love. While Yeats also
asserted the importance of love, he meant by it something
more ardent, sexual, and individualized, less humanitarian, less
cultural than Pound meant. He thought, moreover, that curiosity was too unimpassioned a quality, and that affections which
were too eclectic and international could only diminish imaginative intensity.

Both writers agreed that they lived in an age of decline,
'beastly and cantankerous' for Pound, 'half dead at the top' for
Yeats. ('My dear William B.Y. your 1/2 was too moderate,'
the *Pisan Cantos* admonished.) For Yeats the cure was to
condense and arrange experience. Pound thought this procedure
could only lead to premature synthesis, born from an insufficient
'phalanx of particulars.' For Pound, the cure was to probe, experiment, accumulate until things—some things at any rate—
shone with their intrinsic light: Yeats thought such experimen-
tation might reach no end. Pound's view of experience is as
'improvisatory,' as informalist, as Yeats's is formalist. The city
of the imagination for Yeats is Byzantium, taken by assault; for
Pound it is Fasa, the African city described by Frobenius, built
and patiently built three times again until it becomes 'in the
mind indestructible,' an image of perfection so remote as to

carry that special arcane inflection which is Pound's. But while Fasa is, like Ithaca, essential as journey's end, the incidents on the way to it beset Pound's mind with cryptic relevance or with unresolved irrelevance. Helter-skelter may or may not lead to epiphany; it sometimes exists only because Fasa must confront an opposite, and many varieties of helter-skelter will serve. The lack of inevitability is a guarantee of authenticity, of an honesty not to be gulled by esthetics. Pound's art in the *Cantos* is coagulative, Yeats's in his poems is exploitative; the poets face each other in an unended debate.

V

※》《※

Possum's Conversion

THE COINCIDENCE which recently joined in the same year Yeats's centenary and Eliot's death invokes also their long, languid incompatibility. Among their various mild collisions none was more defined than the dinner at Wellesley College when Yeats, seated next to Eliot but oblivious of him, conversed with the guest on the other side until late in the meal. He then turned and said, 'My friend here and I have been discussing the defects of T. S. Eliot's poetry. What do you think of that poetry?' Eliot held up his place card to excuse himself from the jury.

For Eliot as a young man looking for French ironies, Yeats was ornate and romantic, a protracted Pre-Raphaelite, while for Yeats as an old man, looking for wildness and strangeness, Eliot was too plain, a belated Alexander Pope, making poetry resemble prose. To others as well as to himself Yeats was accustomed to describe Eliot's verse as gray, cold, dry, flat, bare. While acknowledging its effect on the young, he regarded it as counter-revolutionary rather than revolutionary. Eliot, eluding the inheritance of the Hydraulic Press Brick Company of St. Louis, could not forget it. The gashouse and operating table replaced, as Yeats observed without enthusiasm, romantic metaphor, but only to cause Eliot a second aversion. The world became real to Eliot only to the degree that it was revolting. Auden's delight in the machinery of the gashouse, while inexplicable to Yeats, was at any rate a passion for the world and so preferable to Eliot's distaste.

Yeats was also critical of Eliot's Christianity. He thought it for a modern mind unreal. At his most indulgent, he allowed that it might serve Eliot as 'a convenient symbolism for some older or newer thought.' At his most severe, he considered Eliot's religious development a false solution of the contemporary esthetic problem, because it entailed submission rather than search. What was necessary was to map out an 'exposition of intellectual needs' such as Yeats's own *A Vision* provided; instead Eliot surrendered to belief. Yeats thought he saw in Eliot's work the turning of intellect upon itself, so that even when myth was employed, it was held rigidly apart from fact to play (and misplay) two tunes instead of one.

This attitude toward Eliot remained fixed. Eliot's attitude toward Yeats underwent, on the other hand, a curious change. When he arrived in London in 1914, he was not eager to be anyone's disciple, Yeats's least of all. Ezra Pound brought him two or three times into the presence, and Eliot allowed himself only to be bored. Yeats's two subjects of conversation at that period, he said later, were 'George Moore and spooks.' It is hard to know which interested Eliot less. He did not go to Woburn Buildings any more. For several years he thought of Yeats as a leftover from the 'nineties, an out-of-the-way interest of Pound's. Then, at some point, Eliot had to modify his view. There is evidence of punctilious wobbling in Eliot's choice of the date when this climactic recognition occurred. Once he hit on 1916, the year that he attended a performance of Yeats's play, *At the Hawk's Well*, and was surprised by the strength of its diction. His surprise was evidently tempered, however, by the feeling which he also expressed later, that the play did not solve the problem of writing modern verse drama. Nineteen-nineteen is the other year Eliot gives for his having been won over to Yeats, evidently by the volume *The Wild Swans at Coole*. But this date must also be too early, for his review of a book of Yeats's essays in the *Athenaeum* during that year largely dismisses him as 'a foreign mind,' not foreign only to England but to the earth in general, a mind 'in some way independent of experience.' Neither poet agreed with the other's way of walking on the earth. Eliot is stern: 'His remoteness is not an escape from the world, for he is innocent of any world to escape from.' He finds Yeats's mind to be crude and egoistic because of not facing direct contacts, and successful only in achieving solipsism. He returns to the attack in 'A Cooking Egg,' published the following year, where the lines,

> I shall not want Pipit in Heaven:
> Madame Blavatsky will instruct me
> In the Seven Sacred Trances,

may well recall Yeats's stories of his membership in the Blavatsky Lodge.

Eliot's nervous breakdown the following year drove him to Switzerland where, prompted perhaps by the Alpine surroundings, he conflated Himavant and Olivet, Buddha and Christ, in a new synthesis. *The Waste Land* presented a figure like Madame Blavatsky under the name of Madame Sosostris, but this time she was not made entirely a charlatan. Her Tarot cards and the fortunes she elicits from them are vestigial of ancient mysteries. For his plan and much of his incidental symbolism in the poem, Eliot relied as he said on Jessie L. Weston's *From Ritual to Romance* (1920). Miss Weston has little to say about the Tarot, but she quotes a private letter from Yeats to her confirming that the Tarot suits are lasting elements of the mystical tradition and remain the basis of magical practices. Eliot must have

wryly recognized that his own interests in comparative mythology had carried him athwart Yeats's. But instead of using the
Tarot as ancestral to modern magic, he used it as ancestral to
modern religion, arbitrarily (as he specified) associating the
Hanged Man in the pack with Christ. The mysteries concealed
in the Tarot pack become an apocryphal source of the New
Testament. So Eliot, like Miss Weston, brings the pagan mysteries into the central Christian tradition, while Yeats is content
to keep them in the mystical periphery.

That Eliot and Yeats should unexpectedly bow across Miss
Weston's book did not make their relations peaceable, but
Eliot shows a little less impatience and, gradually, a little more
respect. In 1923, reviewing *Ulysses,* he mentions Yeats favorably
for 'adumbrating' what must now be the new method in literature, of manipulating a continuous parallel between contempo-
raneity and antiquity. To adumbrate is, however, not to achieve,
and it is Joyce rather than Yeats who is praised for perfecting
the method. Evidently Eliot was as yet only slightly concessive,
for in 1925 Ezra Pound, who was in a position to know, remarked in a letter, Eliot 'don't see either Yeats or Hardy.' There
is some confirmation of Pound in 1933, when Eliot discussed
Yeats rather patronizingly in lectures eventually published under
the title *After Strange Gods.* Yeats had been guilty of two mis-
takes, Eliot discovered: he had tried to make poetry supplant
religion, and he had tried to fabricate an individual religion.
Eliot supports himself with a remark of I. A. Richards (not
always his ally) that Yeats had repudiated life in favor of a
supernatural world, one insufficiently connected with normal
experience. Eliot could hardly forbid a supernatural enthusiasm,
but Yeats's supernatural world was the wrong one, provincial
and eccentric. He is really still objecting, though in lecture language, to Yeats's spooks. Then, to lighten his attack, Eliot
praises Yeats for having given up most of his eccentricity in his

more recent, austere poetry. He quotes with only partial sympathy—because its subject is regret—one passage from Yeats's poem, 'Vacillation':

> Things said or done long years ago,
> Or things I did not do or say
> But thought that I might say or do,
> Weigh me down, and not a day
> But something is recalled,
> My conscience or my vanity appalled.

And Eliot concludes with evident strain that 'Yeats has arrived at greatness against the greatest odds.' In his last years Eliot rather regretted the whole volume in which this criticism appeared, and would not allow it to be republished.

The seventieth birthday of Yeats in 1935 stirred Eliot to speak more handsomely of him. He devoted a leading article in the *Criterion* to acknowledging Yeats's pre-eminence, and praising especially the terse simplicity of his late diction. Then Yeats's death in 1939 led him to detailed and laudatory summary. In the 'provincial' and 'eccentric' capital he told his Dublin audience that Yeats was 'the greatest poet of our time—certainly the greatest in this language, and so far as I am able to judge, in any language.' He later omitted this praise, perhaps feeling it was fulsome or trite as an obituary. But the rest of his speech, which he kept intact in reprinting, testified to his respect. He takes the opportunity to defend Yeats's poem, 'The Spur,'

> You think it horrible that lust and rage
> Should dance attendance upon my old age;
> They were not such a plague when I was young:
> What else have I to spur me into song?

Eliot comments in the poem's favor, 'To what honest man, old enough, can these sentiments be entirely alien? They can be subdued and disciplined by religion, but who can say that they are dead?' In his conclusion to this essay, Eliot indicates that he finds Yeats's thought and feeling in some aspects unsympathetic, and that there remain vital questions in the field of doctrine, which ultimately affect one's view of the poet. He boggles still, yet has clearly undertaken with conscience the literary experience of learning to like what one does not like.

So it is particularly admirable, after this, to find the figure of Yeats reappearing in Eliot's poetry, in *Little Gidding* (1946). He reappears like one of his own spooks, and in ghostly form converses with Eliot who is patrolling London streets in wartime during an air raid. Though not named, and though, as Eliot said later, the figure blends various writers, especially Yeats and Swift, it is primarily and recognizably Yeats. As if to confirm the article in the *Criterion,* the spirit speaks of his concern with speech, with purifying, in Mallarmé's words, the dialect of the tribe, and associates himself in this with Eliot. Some of the other lines also suggest that Eliot had reached a new and final stage in his onerous relationship with Yeats. The dead poet, no longer aggressive and tormented, warns the living one ironically of what gifts to expect in old age:

> Let me disclose the gifts reserved for age
> 　To set a crown upon your lifetime's effort.
> 　First, the cold friction of expiring sense
> Without enchantment, offering no promise
> 　But bitter tastelessness of shadow fruit
> 　As body and soul begin to fall asunder.
> Second, the conscious impotence of rage
> 　At human folly, and the laceration
> 　Of laughter at what ceases to amuse.
> And last, the rending pain of re-enactment
> 　Of all that you have done, and been; the shame
> 　Of motives late revealed, and the awareness
> Of things ill done and done to others' harm
> 　Which once you took for exercise of virtue.
> 　Then fools' approval stings, and honour stains.

> From wrong to wrong the exasperated spirit
> Proceeds, unless restored by that refining fire
> Where you must move in measure, like a dancer.

In more didactic phrasing to suit the purgatorial scene, Eliot is paraphrasing here not only Yeats's poem on lust and rage, 'The Spur,' but also the other poem on remorse, 'Vacillation,' which he had quoted earlier. There is a further tribute to Yeats in these lines: Eliot uses the images of fire and dance in the way they are used in Yeats's poem, 'Byzantium,' as images of the timeless:

> At midnight on the Emperor's pavement flit
> Flames that no faggot feeds, nor steel has lit,
> Nor storm disturbs, flames begotten of flame,
> Where blood-begotten spirits come
> And all complexities of fury leave,
> Dying into a dance,
> An agony of trance,
> An agony of flame that cannot singe a sleeve.

The disagreements with Yeats over doctrine are forgotten, and nothing is said this time about provinciality or eccentricity. Just as in the third part of Eliot's *The Waste Land* the collocation of Buddha and St. Augustine, representatives of non-Christian and Christian cultures, is, as Eliot says warily in his footnote, 'not accidental,' so the collocation of Yeats and Eliot here is deliberate and marks the reconciliation of their lifelong differences. Eliot thought this last of the *Four Quartets* his best poem, and perhaps one reason for his estimate was that it brought about his rapprochement with the poet who had always been formidably present in his consciousness. True friendship was only possible after Yeats was dead, and could be sifted down to those elements which Eliot found congenial. That he found, at last, so many, is a measure of Yeats's continued sway over the mind.

VI

⊷⊶

Gazebos and Gashouses

THE PUBLIC demeanor of poets toward each other is usually courteous, though it verges on punctilio. But when their private letters are published, posthumously of course, we learn how furious they were with the Nobel Prize committee for overlooking them to favor some inadequate other. The impingement of someone else's poetic world upon theirs also makes them restless, as if their centripetal energy might not suffice to keep them in orbit. Yet as years pass they become accustomed to their rivals, until one of them dies. Then they feel an unexpected regret, for the consequence must be that some unfamiliar competitor, laden with unfamiliar hostility, is likely to replace the late lamented. So they are always eloquent in regretting other poets' deaths, and garrets must be full these days of heartfelt elegies for T. S. Eliot, written by poets who had not a good word to say for him during the last twenty years. The living poet remains a source of vexation for another reason, that it is never certain which of two poets will *write* the elegy, and which *LoL* be its *subject*. The feeling that one poet may some day be fertilizing the other's mournful rhymes clouds the relationship of the living.

These sombre reflections may help to prepare for the relationship between Yeats and Auden. They met only a few times, often enough to recognize that in poetry and thought they were eminent adversaries. More than one generation separated them, for Auden was born forty-two years after Yeats. Auden's mind was forming when Yeats was in his fifties. Looking back, they find the modern period beginning at different times. For Yeats the death of Victoria marks the change, for Auden the First World War.

In the literary rivalries of the 1920s and 1930s, Yeats was a peculiar encumbrance for young poets. Those who went up to Oxford in the late 1920s—Auden, MacNeice, and Spender— were puzzled whether to regard him as a monument or a folly. His intellectual vagaries embarrassed them as being primitive, and if that was not, since the Dadaists, an adequate slur, primitive in the wrong way. And yet the verse of Yeats was cultivated and subtle, not to be scouted or easily matched. Even as an older man he persisted in exploring themes such as personal love and general ruin, themes the young poets would have liked to reserve for themselves. His behavior was much less congenial to them than T. S. Eliot's. Eliot was proceeding with stately anguish into middle age and spirituality, while Yeats advanced precipitously, without this American decorum, upon old age and corporeality.

Eliot, as their leader, and their publisher, had the right to exist, or at least to co-exist. Bridges and Hardy were uncompetitive codgers from whom technical graces or ineptnesses might usefully be borrowed. Hopkins, while highly influential, was safely dead; one might even feel original in discovering him. Yeats, however, remained intrusive. As Auden observes, not altogether without respect, Yeats refused to play the 'twenties game of understatement, or the 'thirties game of Social Concern, games for which Auden himself helped to lay down the rules. He had the effrontery to ignore the modern imagery that others considered *de rigueur*. We can detect three ages of poetry: Eliot

looked at the gasworks and—despaired; Auden pushed past to
go inside and admire the machinery, asking, 'How many horse-
power is the large turbine?' much as Hart Crane, at about the
same time, looked at his father's cannery works and exulted; as
for Yeats, he had long since passed by, thinking of Trojan towers
or of Lissadell gazebos. Or we might compare the poets' behavior
in houses—Eliot appalled by human habitations and by those
who do not own but rent them and crumble with their plaster,
Yeats looking for one grand or noble enough to endorse, Auden
praising the benefits of the American kitchen or the good toilet
in his Austrian house as he probes the significance, immediate
and ulterior, of the common actions we spend our lives in per-
forming. Still, Yeats claimed to have a modern consciousness
too, even if Auden declined to concede the point. Just as in
1900, before Auden was born, Yeats had denounced Bernard
Shaw as a reactionary, because Shaw was caught up in the outmoded scientific epoch, so he was capable of suggesting that
the modern poets were not so progressive as they supposed, but
were cutting back to flat places in human development where
control of environment gave way to barren submission to it.

Auden's attitude to Yeats could not be called sympathetic—
sympathy would be gratuitous as well as insulting—but he tries
to be judicious in an antic way. Since Auden is more outspoken
than most poets, his attitudes enable two phases of modern
poetry to confront each other. He began to speak his mind
about Yeats before Yeats had died. His remarks show impatience of the power play by which Yeats had taken over
English poetry; they vary in their point of attack, as if Auden
saw many vulnerabilities yet had trouble finding the weakest
spot. His first public mention of Yeats appears to be in the verse
'Letter to Lord Byron' which he wrote in Iceland in 1936, by
which time he was twenty-nine and Yeats seventy-one. Auden
informs Byron that poetry is not dead:

> Cheer up! There're several singing birds that sing,
>   There's six feet six of Spender for a start;
> Eliot has really stretched his eagle's wing,
>   And Yeats has helped himself to Parnell's heart.

The allusion to Eliot's eagle wing bows respectfully to a metaphor of Eliot, while the reference to Yeats's eating habits mali-
ciously tumbles one of Yeats's metaphors about. In a little
poem published the previous year Yeats had said that if De
Valera had eaten Parnell's heart, Ireland's imagination would
have been satisfied. Auden, while listing Yeats among the genuine poets, found this image portentous. He is probably also
responsible for the passage about Yeats in the poem signed
jointly by him and MacNeice, their 'Last Will and Testament,'
where they both determine to 'leave the phases of the moon /
To Mr. Yeats to rock his bardic sleep.' We can imagine their
private jokes about poets who set themselves up as bards and
laid claim, as Yeats did, to having a vision. The refusal to be
quite serious about Yeats is one of the forms of their rebellion
against him.

But mockery is, in an inside-out way, a compliment. Another
poem by MacNeice in the same volume registers Yeats's influence much more politely with such lines as,

> There was MacKenna
> Spent twenty years translating Greek philosophy,
> Ill and tormented, unwilling to bread contract,
> A brilliant talker who left
> The salon for the solo flight of Mind,

lines which evoke the troubled spirits of Yeats's 'All Souls'
Night.' As for Auden, if we compare his first book, *Poems*
(1928), with any of Yeats's early books, they prove surprisingly
alike in theme. Both poets concentrate their attention upon the
antiphony of unsuccess in love and decline in the world. With

Yeats the reverberations are felt in the spheres ('dishevelled wandering stars') while with Auden they are likelier to express themselves in the dream of 'a buried engine-room.' Yeats makes unrequited love a symbol of human aspiration and limit, while Auden, disdaining Yeats's early vocabulary, dwells upon transitoriness of feeling (both for the lover and the beloved), and reviles love as a 'dishonest country,' 'a delicious lie,' 'brief adherence,' 'obsolete or extremely rare.' When, in the poem later entitled 'The Letter,' that disappointing communication arrives, it is made part of a canvas of general thwart:

> Nor speech is close, nor fingers numb
> If love not seldom has received
> An unjust answer, was deceived;
> I, decent with the seasons, move
> Different or with a different love,
> Nor question overmuch the nod,
> The stone smile of this country god,
> That never was more reticent,
> Always afraid to say more than it meant.

It is the world of Humphrey Bogart. Like his, the brave words about seasonal passion conceal both considerable anguish and an inner capacity for fidelity and intensity which, rather than acknowledge, the poet would pretend does not exist. The necessary obverse of this seeming derogation of love is in Auden's poems soon afterwards, where love becomes the animating principle of the world, 'the interest itself in thoughtless heaven.' Having got love away from Yeats, and from Petrarch, Auden is free to capitalize and mythologize it once again, as flagrantly as they would do. The country god once so reticent re-opens his mouth.

In the last few years Auden has regretted some tendencies of his early work: 'It is not the fault of Yeats or Rilke that I allowed myself to be seduced by them into writing poems which were false to my personal and poetic nature.' He attributes to his middle age an increasing revulsion to the 'element of "theatre," of exaggerated gesture and fuss, of indifference to the naked truth.' This revulsion was present, however, at the time that the Yeats influence was at its strongest. Already as a young man of twenty and twenty-one, when he wished to speak with an authority comparable to Yeats's on kindred subjects, he sensed that his own style was powerful enough to filter Yeats's lines and make them his own. For instance, he describes how, in company with his beloved, he watched buzzards as they swept down the sky:

> I, though a watcher too,
> Saw little where they sped.
> Who could have dreamed that you
> Would turn your head?

The stanza probably echoes a couplet from an early poem of Yeats:

> O heart! O heart! if she'd but turn her head,
> You'd know the folly of being comforted.

Auden fastens on the immediate physical gesture, which he leaves a little enigmatic since it may signify either love renewed or carrion love. For Yeats the turning of the head is totally figurative, like the word 'heart.' Auden permits emblematic gestures to retain something undeciphered as if it were a guarantee of actuality.

Another poem of Auden shows, Stephen Spender has noted, that Auden had been reading Yeats's 'The Tower,' which had just then (in 1928) been published. But again the effect is one of filtering. Yeats had written,

> I choose upstanding men
> That climb the streams until
> The fountain leap, and at dawn

> Drop their cast at the side
> Of dripping stone,

and the scene is instantly eternal. Auden begins more matter-of-factly,

> I chose this lean country
> For seven day content,
> To satisfy the want
> Of eye and ear, to see
> The slow fastidious line
> That disciplines the fell,
> A curlew's creaking call
> From angles unforeseen,
> The drumming of a snipe,
> Surprise where driven sleet
> Had scalded to the bone
> And streams were acrid yet
> To an unaccustomed lip . . .

Eternity is expressly denied, for this is a place of seven-day content, a holiday not a Great Year. The word 'unaccustomed' attracts Auden as much as the word 'accustomed' attracts Yeats. When Auden speaks of 'eye and ear,' he is echoing other lines from 'The Tower,' 'Nor an ear and eye / That more expected the impossible,' but he is beset rather by the possible. 'The slow fastidious line / That disciplines the fell,' is a brilliant adaptation of three lines from 'In Memory of Major Robert Gregory,'

> . . . cold Clare rock and Galway rock and thorn,
> Of that stern colour and that delicate line
> That are our secret discipline.

Auden makes his presence felt by changing 'delicate' to 'fastidious' and limiting that word with 'slow,' a combination of adjectives that Yeats might have considered only at the very end of his career. The word 'discipline,' in Yeats always a noun, seems as a verb to come from prose rather than from poetry. One of

Auden's great achievements is to bring a new tenseness to the relations of these two modes. Again there is a difference in gravity: Auden finds the conjunction of art and nature more accidental and less integral with his own style; it is only one of several equally cogent morals offered by an obliging landscape. He is unwilling to grant so much iconic prestige, or iconic singlemindedness, to what he observes.

The poem continues to allude to Yeats, and to subvert him, as it goes on,

> And sitting by the fall
> Spoke with a poet there
> Of Margaret the brazen leech,
> And that severe Christopher,
> Of such and such and such and such
> Till talk tripped over love,
> And both dropped silent in
> The contemplation of
> A singular vision
> And sceptical beholder . . .
> A blackbird's sudden scurry
> Lets broken treetwigs fall
> To shake the torpid pool . . .

[handwritten margin notes: Adam's Curse; Wallace Stevens]

Auden has in mind 'The Secrets of the Old,'

> How such a man pleased women most
> Of all that are gone,
> How such a pair loved many years
> And such a pair but one,

as well as a number of Yeats's birds, notably that mentioned at the end of 'The Tower,'

> Or a bird's sleepy cry
> Among the deepening shades.

In Yeats the talk of love is unifying, while in Auden it enforces a separation; in Yeats the mental experience which the bird culminates is so overwhelming as to make irrelevant the previous identification of his bird's species, while Auden's blackbird, imparting a comparable message of endurance, seems to exist apart from the meaning imposed upon it by the poem. Yeats is always moving from particulars to the universal; of many examples, the most extraordinary comes in 'The Tower,'

> I pace upon the battlements and stare
> On the foundations of a house, or where
> Tree, like a sooty finger, starts from the earth,

where 'tree' exists as undifferentiated, having neither genus nor even an article to precede it. Auden's symbols are less fixed and inevitability is not claimed for them.

After Yeats's death in 1939 Auden made several efforts to sort out his mixed feelings about the dead poet's mysterious interfusion into the period. He has written five articles on Yeats in prose. Among them one is a review of *Last Poems*, summing them up with some distaste (a distaste shared with Eliot) for their old-goatishness, one is a mock-trial for *Partisan Review*, entitled 'The Public v. the Late William Butler Yeats,' in which Auden shared his divided thoughts among prosecution and defense. Another is a paper, 'Yeats as an Example,' which praises him on technical grounds for releasing the lyric from 'iambic monotony,' and on substantive grounds for introducing serious reflections into occasional poems, though it does not endorse any of the serious reflections themselves. When he came to write about Yeats's *Letters* for the *New Yorker*, Auden had prepared himself for rodomontade, and was unusually indulgent when he found that Yeats was fully capable of self-mockery. But in reviewing *Mythologies* for a book club, Auden protested sharply against Yeats's refusal to distinguish between faith and myth, between what was true and what was just traditional.

He has also memorialized Yeats in two poems, one an elegy,

the other a limerick, as if he could not think of Yeats except in two conflicting ways. The limerick offers advice for students:

> To get the Last Poems of Yeats
> You need not mug up on dates;
> All a reader requires
> Is some knowledge of gyres
> And the sort of people he hates.

The elegy, 'In Memory of W. B. Yeats,' must be unique among elegies in English in that it takes its subject to task even while expressing admiration for his example. It has little to say of regret; may there not be in it even a minuscule touch of relief? It is hard to be sure, because Auden's method in elegy as in love lyric is to underline all that we must not say. Yet he does take the occasion of death to put the poet into manageable proportions, and to alert us to the shortcomings as well as the virtues of the deceased.

The first of the poem's three parts begins, 'He disappeared in the dead of winter,' and chills the climate to suit his theme, for it is the climate in which Auden heard of the death, not that in which Yeats died at Roquebrune. He soon declares, 'O all the instruments agree / The day of his death was a dark, cold day.' No epic personages show up, only the barometer is invoked as expert witness. In allowing scientific instruments to express themselves, Auden may be unconsciously underscoring his own freedom from what he noted elsewhere to be a flaw, the failure of Yeats to relate his outlook to science. But chiefly Auden is being himself; he prefers to present himself, as if otherwise he might become dishonest, in the guise of a grieving computer. His instruments were at first allowed, nevertheless, a good deal of emotion: Auden prefixed the threnodic word 'O' to their concurring reports, and the sudden strong rhythm implies what is left unsaid, that Yeats's death is a dark cold blow. In the most recent version of the poem, Auden (like Yeats an inveterate

reviser) says, 'What instruments we have agree,' as if their testi-
mony might not be totally reliable, and as if the previous version
had been too easily ironic, or had anthropomorphized machinery. The new line almost suppresses the machines, though
it tilts toward the opposite danger in Auden, of making restraint
sound doctrinaire.

As we know from other works of Auden, such as 'Musée des
Beaux Arts,' he liked to point out to a generation prone to
pathetic fallacy how indifferent surrounding objects are to
human activities. An emotion is rendered more poignant by
observing creatures and things that have ignored it. This studied
irrelevancy is a tactic that he shares with Robbe-Grillet: the
portrayal of truth by evoking and putting aside a false context.
But in this elegy Auden has a special reason. The wolves continued—regardless of the poet's death—to run through the ever-
green forests; paradise was still unregained, and the peasant river
was untempted by the fashionable quays, as if to suggest that
the class barrier which Yeats thought to surmount, between the
peasantry and 'hard-riding country gentlemen,' was fixed regardless of the poet's embrace of both groups. So far it seems that
Yeats has merely failed, as (Auden thinks) all poets must, but
the next conceit is as complimentary as it is accurate: 'By mourning tongues / The death of the poet was kept from his poems.'
Nature is still nature, the classes still persist, but the poems,
now as inevitable in the landscape as trees or rivers, survive their
maker's disappearance. Bent on avoiding insincerity as well as
fulsomeness, Auden finds what may be said genuinely about
Yeats's death is that the earth's axle did not break, but that a
few thousand will think of this day as of a day when one did
something slightly unusual. All the panoply of mourning is
subdued, and the panoply of a poet's greatness is put into terms
that even a generation skeptical of the reach of poetic genius
can accept.

The second part of the poem registers certain complaints against Yeats, comradely complaints. In prose Auden had written that Yeats was 'not conspicuously intelligent,' and now he softens that blow a little, 'You were silly like us.' In the *New Republic*, where the first version of the elegy was published, this line was in the third person, 'He was silly like us; his gift survived it all,' but Auden then decided to speak directly to Yeats, and to itemize some of the sillinesses. He considers Yeats's poetic motivation to have come from Irishism: 'Mad Ireland hurt you into poetry,' and then he points out that Ireland, for all Yeats's efforts, remains as mad as ever. Now he is led to his own conclusion, expressed in a prose article before being inserted in the poem, 'For poetry makes nothing happen; it is instead / A way of happening, a mouth.' This apothegm is really a rebuke to the dead poet, for Yeats, as Auden knew, could not stomach the view that poetry was ineffectual, even if splendidly so. It is also questionable in itself, since events cannot be separated from the emotions to which they give birth, nor roused human feelings from subsequent events.

The debate with this formidable corpse continues into the third and final section of the poem, where Auden originally said that Yeats, like Claudel and, of all poets, Kipling, would be pardoned at last because he used language so well. In one of his essays Auden suggests that Yeats's diction was the diction of a just man, even if some of his opinions were unjust—and such a defense may yet prove the best against the multiplying accusations that Yeats was a fascist; here, however, Auden is interested in attesting good poetry as if it could be distinct from good character. The comparison of an Irish nationalist with a British imperialist is casual, and shows the dangers of an apothegmatic style. Auden quickly became aware of these dangers himself, and he has dropped these three stanzas from the elegy in recent editions, although anthologies still reprint them. Yeats was in fact scarcely in need of such a defense, or of any sort of pardon, even one granted by Time.

Only in the last verses does Auden praise without qualification one attribute, that Yeats celebrated life amid public and private ruin, and so to the inhabitants of a fallen world presented reminders of Eden. If poetry really possesses so much power over men's minds as this, it would seem much more instrumental in life than Auden had earlier admitted. Auden's own poetry, which was full of threats of doom and revolution in the 1930s, has shifted since then to finding things to live rather than to die for. In endorsing Yeats's celebrative gift, he may be bespeaking a turn in his own verse as well.

The mixed feelings which underlie his elegy confirm a pattern of divergence between the two poets which is also present in their biographies. They were grandsons of Episcopalian ministers, though Yeats's grandfather was low church and Auden's high church. Auden's family remained devout through the next generation, while Yeats's father was a skeptic. Auden, described by Isherwood as in childhood startlingly high church, lost his religious belief in adolescence, to regain it in his thirties; he has recently delivered a sermon in Westminster Abbey. Yeats had little interest in Christianity after his early childhood. He was not an iconoclast, however, but worked out his own iconography in which he conferred on Christianity an especially modest role.

For Yeats, who had spent much of his childhood in Sligo, the ideal landscape was always the pastoral one; looking out at a beautiful Italian countryside with Ezra Pound, Yeats remarked that it was 'Sligo in heaven.' Auden has always preferred another setting, that of the industrial Midlands; his favorite scenic route was the one from Birmingham to Wolverhampton. If Yeats liked lakes, Auden was partial to 'tramlines and slag-heaps, pieces of machinery.' I'm not sure how to interpret the fact that Yeats liked towers and Auden lead mines, but—Freud

dirty joke

apart—and yet not to give up too easily—these propensities may
suggest that Yeats was always struggling to be more than his
ordinary self, with a consequent imagery of high places, of
figures larger than life—while Auden was pitched lower, struggling to comprehend the self's buried workings or, as he said,
'with prolonged drowning to develop gills.' Masking pleased the
one as much as unmasking, the other. While Yeats studied mystical ways to expand consciousness and control the mind, Auden
pored over his father's anatomy and pathology books.

   Their poetic development also sets them at variance. Yeats's
first masters were Rossetti and Morris, mellifluous Pre-Raphael-
ites. Auden's first master was Thomas Hardy, the sore thumb
of late nineteenth-century poets. Auden chose to be influenced
by Old English poetry, Yeats by Old Irish sagas; at first Yeats
tended to prettify the ancient material, but he gradually grew
tougher, while Auden was tough from the start. In later life
Yeats, originally so gracious, became vehement, while Auden, so
consciously awkward at first, writes now (even when translating
the Eddas) with more suavity. Yeats's early verse suffers from
an excess of connectives like 'and,' while Auden's is characterized by a lack of them, but both poets grew tired of their
chosen mannerisms. One poet they share as a common ancestor,
William Blake, but they find different things in him to admire:
Auden, who calls himself a 'lunatic clergyman,' liked especially
Blake's moral revolution, while Yeats took up also Blake's deliberate symbolism and eccentric metaphysics. Auden refused to
follow, for like Eliot he found Blake in these regions as ex-
asperating as Yeats.

   What exactly was the core of Auden's exasperation with his
older contemporary? There was first, as he says in 'Yeats as an
Example,' that interest in Celtic mythology and occult symbolism. To relate these two is symptomatic, since they have no
necessary connection; Auden finds them both tiresomely pro-

vincial. He complains with mock-snobbery that they are not 'the kind of nonsense that can be believed by a gentleman.' He calls Yeats's interest in the occult 'Southern Californian,' and elsewhere connects it with the psychology of the *rentier* class, at its most powerful in England during the time that Yeats was being artistically formed. This economic determinism might be more persuasive if occultism had not been equally powerful in other countries where different economic conditions prevailed, most notably France. It may be that Auden himself has not totally escaped this infection, for when Stravinsky was collaborating with him on *The Rake's Progress*, the composer was startled to learn that his librettist believed in graphology, astrology, the telepathic power of cats, black magic as described in Charles Williams's novels, in categories of temperament (Stravinsky, because he happened to work at night, was booked as a Dionysian), in pre-ordination, in Fate. Auden disavows some of Stravinsky's listings: while he believes in graphology, he doesn't in astrology. He believes in the power of cats, not as telepathy but as an 'understanding of human discourse and gesture.' He thinks black magic possible, but something one shouldn't touch, 'either childish and silly or dangerous to sanity and salvation.' Perhaps we are all occultists a little. But in his work, Auden includes the occult only to overcome it. In this he is opposite to Yeats. The medium in Yeats's play *The Words upon the Window-Pane* is suspected of being a fraud but in the end is shown to have incontrovertible clairvoyant power; while in Auden's and Kallman's *Elegy for Young Lovers*, a woman who sees visions is successfully cured of seeing them. In a similar way, the mirrorlike crystal in *The Ascent of F6* lays bare not secrets of the preternatural but traumas of childhood. There are ghosts, but they are within us, and we must get them out, Auden seems to say. They are outside us, says Yeats, and we must take them in.

To such complaints as Auden's, Yeats had answers ready. Provincialism, so distasteful to Auden, was something Yeats sought; he wished to bind emotions to what was local, both in landscape and in traditional images. Moreover he wanted to make his province the world, rather than like Auden, a more consistent traveler, to make the world his province. As for occultism, not every quiver or shudder had to be defended as a genuine expression of the timeless. Yeats believed in the imagination, and held that it had links with a collective mind which could not be explained in terms of scientific psychology. Auden is usually chary of using the word imagination, and prefers to say that everyone is 'from time to time excited emotionally and intellectually by his social and material environment,' and that this excitement 'in certain individuals produces verbal structures which we call poems.' This diction was foreign to Yeats, who preferred to be taken in by imaginative nonsense because he was attracted to it, rather than to reject it because most people were not. He could also have maintained that he was in his supernatural beliefs much less dogmatic than Auden, in his later phase of revived Christian feeling, has become. Auden would have sternly replied, I suppose, that there was no virtue in stickling at the wrong dogma.

Auden also finds fault with Yeats's literary theories. He fervently opposes Yeats's claims for the importance of poetry, and maintains that they are extravagant and dated. When Yeats declares,

> The intellect of man is forced to choose
> Perfection of the life, or of the work,

Auden comments: 'This is untrue; perfection is possible in neither.' This belief has not however prevented his admittedly composing (with Kallman) the *Elegy for Young Lovers* on the theme here unwittingly proffered by Yeats. When Yeats asks, in 'Sailing to Byzantium,' to be turned after death into what Auden calls a mechanical bird, Auden, while granting the stanza's 'utmost magnificence,' feels that Yeats is telling 'what my nanny would have called "a story." ' When Yeats writes in 'Under Ben Bulben,'

> Cast a cold eye
> On life, on death.
> Horseman, pass by,

Auden says the horseman is a stage prop; a motorist would be more likely.* When Yeats remarks of 'The Scholars' that

> Bald heads forgetful of their sins,
> Old, learned, respectable bald heads
> Edit and annotate the lines
> That young men, tossing on their beds,
> Rhymed out in love's despair, . . .

Auden rushes to the scholars' defense, 'Thank God they do. If it had not been for scholars working themselves blind copying and collating manuscripts, how many poems would be unavailable . . . and how many others full of lines that made no sense?' Auden obviously regards Yeats as a balloonist and himself as the man with the pins, an Oxford Yankee at King Cuchullain's court. That he is not merely indulging a hostility to Yeats is proven by his pricking balloons of his own, as when he struck from the poem, 'September 1, 1939,' the stanza ending, 'We must love one another or die,' and explained as his reason, 'We'll die anyway.' He has since struck out the whole poem, because the assumption of total responsibility for the behavior of both the Nazis and the Allies is as foreign to his nature as would be the disclaimer of responsibility for either Germany or England which Yeats's Irish airman professes. Auden displays

---

* But Yeats is probably addressing the ghostly horseman whom he evoked at the beginning of that poem.

always a loyalty to the common elements of living, and is ready to catch himself short when he finds he has played 'Major Prophet.'

His deflations of Yeats depend upon an initial disagreement; he finds Yeats esthetic when he should be ethical, and objects to the esthetic life as an immersion in particulars, a failure to choose the Word instead of just words, and in sum, an abandonment to make-believe. He thinks Yeats prefers, as he himself did sometimes in his early work, sound to sense, and is indifferent to truth, being too much the poet, too little the citizen. Nowhere is the difference plainer than in the prose criticism by the two men of Shakespeare, and particularly of Richard II. To Auden, Richard is an example of the unjust ruler. Of the five qualities which Auden, who loves to rig up lists (though he avoids the kind of apotheosis of lists to be found in Yeats's phases of the moon), prescribes for the just ruler, poor Richard is lacking in four. Prince Hal, on the other hand, has all five and therefore becomes Shakespeare's ideal king. Yeats knew this point of view, or one like it, from earlier criticism, and he disputes it on every count. He refuses to concede that Shakespeare had any serious interest in statecraft, or that he judged men 'with the eyes of a Municipal Councillor weighing the merits of a Town Clerk.' He insists that Shakespeare understood Richard to be ill-fitted for kingship but preferred him to Henry V, as a boy of fine temperament with weak muscles might be preferred to an athletic lunkhead. So Shakespeare endows Richard with lyricism and Henry with the rhetoric of a leading article. Yeats dismisses any idea that Henry was, after all, successful, for he points out that in the cycle of historical plays Henry's son lost everything that had been seemingly won. 'Shakespeare watched Henry V,' says Yeats, 'not indeed as he watched the greater souls in the visionary procession, but cheerfully, as one watches some handsome spirited horse, and he spoke his tale, as he spoke all tales, with tragic irony.' Yeats's Shakespeare is on the side of sensitive anarchy, while Auden's is boisterously law-abiding.

Auden's conception of poetry parallels Eliot's anti-Wordsworthian definition of it as 'a superior amusement.' 'If you call it anything else you are likely to call it something still more false,' Eliot said. In his essay, 'Squares and Oblongs,' Auden denominated poetry an impersonal game, though he quickly adds that the game is one of knowledge, a game in which the fun consists in naming hidden relationships. Elsewhere he defines a game as 'any action or series of actions that can be done perfectly.' Monroe Spears calls attention to a recent statement that all occupations except those of the unskilled workman and the priest are games, requiring special gifts. In both remarks the frivolity of the game is undercut by the demand for skill and the struggle for perfection, which make the game deadly. Auden remains unsettled whether this perfection in poems is possible or not, but he is firm enough in his desire to shun nobler epithets, and the game's stringent requirements raise it to a super-game, 'a timeless world of pure play,' and at the same time a liberation 'from self-enchantment and deception.'

At the end of 'The Enchaffèd Flood' he belittles his art once again, as if he were surrounded by idolaters of it. The artist can neither have such a heroic importance as the romantics supposed, nor can he believe in the Art God enough to desire it. We must not think too well of art, he says as he had said before, and now he adds that we must not confuse it with religion. But his attitude toward art antedates his religious conversion, and seems in fact to go back to his childhood when, he tells us, he excluded magic from his childhood games. Now he shakes his finger and says we must recognize dogma again as the foundation for reason and emotion, not their contradiction. This is pious and utterly unlike Yeats.

In *The Sea and the Mirror*, his commentary on Shakespeare's *Tempest*, Auden has occasionally echoed Yeats, as in his youth, so as to disagree with him. Yeats in 'The Tower' had asked, 'Oh may the moon and sunlight seem / One inextricable beam, / For if I triumph I must make men mad.' Auden characteristically takes up Prospero at the moment when he has given up magic, because now, 'I shall just be getting to know / The difference between moonshine and daylight.' Auden shows Antonio withstanding Prospero as art god by holding on to his own intransigency and privacy, somewhat as Judas in Yeats's *Calvary* turns against God to express not disbelief but his own identity and free will. Auden wishes to demonstrate that art is not omnipotent, while Yeats indicates that God is not omnipotent and that man is splendidly unsubdued. At other points the two are not so divergent: that beyond art there is something which Caliban can call 'unrectored chaos' seems to jibe with Yeats's evocations of darkness in his last poems, and that art offers 'feebly figurative signs' of a 'Wholly Other Life' would suit Yeats too, though he would reject *feebly* and say outright that works of art 'all heavenly glory symbolise.' But for Auden the artist's work is essentially a cunning yet relatively helpless effort to cope with nature or experience. For Yeats art and nature have more revelations to offer, and art is essentially a dialectic between nature—whether revelatory or not—and what Kant calls 'second nature,' the artist's own creation from elements nature supplies. This dialectic considers many possibilities, that art depends upon nature, that it interpenetrates nature, that it is powerless in nature, that it shapes nature (as Wilde liked to say), that it transcends nature, and it conceives of nature variously as a temple of symbols or as what Stevens calls 'one insoluble lump' without ulterior meaning.

Auden is aware of this dialectic in Yeats, and uses it a little himself, with less freedom because of his walling off art from religion. He excludes certain possibilities, though he allows art, besides its esthetic attractions, a certain ethical color, achieved by stripping away illusions and by being kind. In this careful reduction of the status of poetry there is perhaps a wilful self-disparagement, a personal humility gratuitously extended to his art. He presents himself as cutting through folderol. In his early poetry he achieved this effect by being abrupt, by snubbing euphony for dissonance, by insisting that the new password for poetry was enigmatic bluntness rather than, as in the early Yeats, enigmatic beauty. He is pleasantly unintimidated by Yeats, though he often seems to be struggling to maintain his own truculent consistency beyond the need for it. Essentially he wishes to characterize two schools of poetry.

We may join in this attempt too. Yeats did belong to a different persuasion from Auden, less offhand, more peremptory. To call poetry a game, even in an understatement which means that it is secretly, or at least occasionally, more than that, would be inconceivable for him. We can imagine his replying to Auden as he liked to remember Berkeley's replying to Hume, 'We Irish do not hold with this.' He did not concede that poetry and religion had portioned up the creation, or that poetry was subordinate to dogma. He said rather that the priest was the poet's shadow, and he meant that the religions of the world expressed in 'gutturals' what the poets had expressed in 'heavenly labials.' And if Auden had reservations about Yeats, Yeats also had reservations about Auden. In fact, as his letters reveal, Yeats thought of the preface to his *Oxford Book of Modern Verse* as an answer to the question, 'How far do I like the Ezra, Eliot, Auden school and if I do not, why not?' and then, since he evidently knew the answer to that one, he added the further question, 'Why do the younger generation like it so much? What do they see or hope?' Auden, momentarily forgetting that writing poems was all a game, in turn referred to

Yeats's anthology as 'the most deplorable volume ever issued'
under the fine Clarendon imprint. (Years afterwards he was
mollified to discover in Yeats's letters that Yeats spoke there
of his poetry with more liking, though with the appalling vagueness of classifying Auden in the 'Cambridge school.' *) In his
late plays, *The Herne's Egg* and *Purgatory,* Yeats seems to be
attempting some Auden-like abruptnesses in the minor characters' speech (he called it fancifully 'sprung verse'), and in his
last prose work, *On the Boiler,* he took occasion to agree with
The Ascent of F6 that monastic abnegation and Western energy
are the two alternatives available now to us.

Yeats's objections to Auden can be found in the preface to the
Oxford Book, in a talk he gave for the B.B.C. on 'Modern
Poetry,' and in his essay, 'A General Introduction to My Work.'
He understood that to the young he appeared to be purveying
'antiquated romantic stuff,' and that literature was seeking a
new direction. More important than his opposition to that
direction was his skill in prognosticating it. With Auden promi-
nently in mind, he complained that these young English poets
'reject drama and personal emotion; they have thought out
opinions that join them to this or that political party; they em-
ploy an intricate psychology, action in character, not as in the
ballads, character in action, and all consider that they have a
right to the same close attention that men pay to the mathe-
matician and the metaphysician. One of the more distinguished
has just explained that man has hitherto slept but must now
wake. They are determined to express the factory, the metrop-
olis, that they may be modern.' Remembering that Auden had
been teaching school for five years, Yeats went on, 'Young men
teaching school in some picturesque cathedral town ... defend
their type of metaphor by saying that it comes naturally to a

* Yeats used Oxford and Cambridge interchangeably in the Oxbridge
fashion.

man who travels to his work by Tube. . . . As they express not what the Upanishads call "that ancient Self" but individual intellect, they have the right to choose the man in the Tube because of his objective importance. They attempt to kill the whale, push the Renaissance higher yet, outthink Leonardo; their verse kills the folk ghost and yet would remain verse. I am joined to the "Irishry" and I expect a counter-Renaissance.' Yeats's statement is as always so figurative as to be variously interpretable, but if he means, as he appears to mean, that the new poets are introducing a flat rationality, he is unjust to that strong sense of the uncanny which, while often masked in Auden by Freudian pseudo-explanation, is always prominent in his early work.

What would Yeats have said if he had had to memorialize Auden instead of Auden's memorializing him? No doubt his portrait of Auden would have become ennobled to the point of archetype, almost beyond recognition. But if Yeats had written in prose, he might have wished Auden to be sillier, or as he might have said, to be more that 'wild old wicked man' whom he presented as his own late image. The claim of being reasonable and honest did not impress him, for Yeats felt that 'poets were good liars who never forgot that the Muses were women who liked the embrace of gay warty lads.' Nor would Yeats have endorsed Auden's affection for the middle style, or, as Marianne Moore more aptly renames it, 'the circumspectly audacious.' If Auden was suspicious of Yeats's later flirtations with aristocracy and even fascism, Yeats was suspicious of Auden's early associations with Communism; it was for Auden's school, he said, a deus ex machina, a Santa Claus, offering a happy ending. His own preference, he says, was for tragedy rather than tragicomedy. The zeal for social change meant an attenuation of personality (a word of which Yeats could still, before the Second World War, be fond) because poets, instead of flaunting their

selves and seeking identification with their opposites, sought
identification with mass movements. When Auden uses the
word 'we,' he means all humanity, while when Yeats uses the
same pronoun he means a limited and elect community.

To Auden's criticism of his mythology as *rentier*, Yeats would
have responded that Auden's theology was equally middle-class,
and had the further taint of being British. I don't know what
Yeats would have made of Auden's change of nationality, from
English to American, but if he had indicated more than amusement he would perhaps have taken it for another indication of a
mind brusque with its own past as with much tradition. He
would not have been pleased by Auden's rejection of the theory
that imagination plays its role in the history of the world, and
that events are in fact best understood as chains of images, often
first generated by poets or by men capable of living at a poetic
pitch. In *The King's Threshold*, an early play which reads like a
dramatic demonstration of Yeats's essays 'The Symbolism of
Poetry' and 'Magic,' the poet Seanchan declares that because
the poets have christened gold, kings have appeared to wear the
crown, and in a late poem, 'The Man and the Echo,' Yeats
remorsefully questions himself about the effect of *Cathleen ni
Houlihan*, 'Did that play of mine send out / Certain men the
English shot?' And it is apparent that the answer is yes, that the
Easter Rebellion stemmed from images which Yeats's patriotic
play helped to generate in men's minds. Auden would insist, 'Art
is not life, and cannot be / A midwife to society,' but Irishmen
in the audience, who felt their national feeling suddenly con-
scripted and marshaled, have testified that Yeats's play did affect
them in this way.

Yeats's view of poetry as working like a subterranean force to
alter men's lives does not sentimentalize its effects as necessarily
virtuous or humanitarian. 'When did the poets promise safety,
King?' asks the poet in *The King's Threshold*. He would agree

with Stevens that 'poetry is a destructive force.' In temerariously
excluding Wilfred Owen from the *Oxford Book of Modern
Verse* (he said in a letter that Owen was 'all blood, dirt, and
sucked sugar-stick') and Sean O'Casey's *The Silver Tassie* from
the Abbey Theatre repertoire (he found it 'anti-war propaganda'),
Yeats made clear that for him poetry, or indeed any art, cannot
find its end in pity. It expresses a more volcanic energy, and its
consciousness of this Blake-like energy enables poetry to cry
out in joy when everything about it falls in ruin.

Yet in espousing the cause of art Yeats is aware of the conse-
quences. He characteristically puts his statement of poetry's
power in the form of a remorseful question rather than of a
flat declaration. Not that less is being claimed—Yeats's conception of poetry is here as radical as Shelley's, though in its dialectical range it also includes the sour and un-Shelleyan recognition (as in 'Byzantium') that poetical flames cannot singe a
sleeve—but there is more modulated assertion, as if the poet,
despairing of other forms of persuasion, drew us, half-startled
and not quite of the same mind, into his own perplexities.
Confuting the notion that poetry is ineffectual, he here suggests
its insidious, demonic power. Auden argues against Shelley that
not the poets, but the secret police, are the unacknowledged
legislators of the world; Yeats's contention is rather that poets
are the world's unacknowledged agitators, continually troubling
the actual with the aspirant. Auden likes to regard the poet as
an averter of panic, a member of the fire brigade, praise which
he accords to Eliot—who appropriately was a fire warden—in
his poem on the latter's sixtieth birthday. He is as comfortable
in praising Eliot as he seems uncomfortable in praising Yeats,
for Eliot preceded him in conversion to the Anglican Church,
though it must be said that Eliot's religious verse is more
painful than Auden's and reconciles piety and poetry, esthetics
and religion, in a way Auden has contravened. Auden's own

Christian poetry tends toward a recognition of general guilt
rather than of individual ecstasy.

✳   But for Yeats the poet does not put out fires, he starts them.
He is a conflagrationist. Auden wants to get a grip on things as
they are, Yeats to reshape them so they take on new properties.
He is interested in flagrancy while Auden is interested in appre-
hension. Their treatment of love suggests the difference in attitude. Maud Gonne seems essential to Yeats's view of things;
some overwhelming defeated passion is needed to agitate the
✳ mind to its extremities. In Auden such fanfare over disappointment would be excessive; he finds it in Yeats a bit 'literary'; his
own love poems, we have noted, emphasize that amorous feeling is 'half-humbug and half true,' they applaud love but insist
upon the painful awareness that time wrings the feelings and
diverts them. He speaks more of friendship than love, and, it
may be, sets more store by it. Auden moves away from explosion,
as since Hiroshima all have moved, while Yeats is always moving
toward it. Auden, as if turning Yeats inside out, has made himself the spokesman for all the things that are not included in
this overmastering passion.

Their views constitute a running dialogue, formulated by
them more or less in this way:

YEATS: I believe in the poet's evocation of disembodied powers
    which, assuming form through the mind, effect changes in
    the world. The proper metaphor for poetry is magic.
AUDEN: Poetry is not magic. Insofar as it has an ulterior purpose,
    this is, by telling the truth, to disenchant and disintoxicate.
YEATS: Truth is the dramatic expression of the highest man, of
    the poet as hero.
AUDEN: The poet no longer fancies himself a hero; he is an ex-
    plorer of possibility.
YEATS: Say impossibility rather.

AUDEN: All that is passé with the romantic movement, thank God. Crying has gone out and the cold bath has come in.

YEATS: The whale is extinct and the little fish lie gasping on the strand.

AUDEN: The artist no longer wanders about in exile, he builds irrigation ditches like Faust in his old age, he votes in elections.

YEATS: The artist has much more in common with the flood than with irrigation. He breaks out of every social dam or political enclosure.

AUDEN: You belong to the school of Mallarmé; you think of yourself as a god who creates the subjective universe out of nothing.

YEATS: You belong to the school of Locke; you split the world into fragments and then worship the cutting edge.

AUDEN: Your world is a chimera.

YEATS: Yours is an urban renewal project.

Before the poets became too heated, perhaps we may try to placate them a little. Yeats is apt to say more than he means, Auden to say less. Yeats regarded himself as a romantic—a school which, like Eliot, Auden professes to detest; yet the bold positions which Yeats shares with romantic poets appear in his verse often with a modern wariness and qualification. They are outposts flung up with a keen sense of imperilment. Auden regards himself as a classicist, yet that term implies a much more settled manner and matter than his work displays. He may be described more profitably as an anti-romantic within the romantic tradition. In a recent poem he declares that he would have liked to sing 'In the old grand manner / Out of a resonant heart,' but that he has been forced by the debasement of words and values to adopt 'the wry, the sotto-voce, / Ironic and monochrome.' It is not like Auden to blame the age for his style, and in fact from the start he has clearly preferred to reject the idealization of art and the manner that accompanies it. Yet at moments he has not been adamant. In *The Sea and the Mirror* Prospero asks Ariel to show in his mirror what Nature is for ever, and when he does so, says, 'one peep ... will be quite enough.' But if the mirror of art can show even one peep at nature in its eternal form, then it must be more powerful than he customarily allows. In his last prose book, *The Dyer's Hand*, Auden for the first time repeatedly emphasizes that poetry is a rite, surrounded with awe. Instead of limiting it to an engaging but futile game, he has it subtly remaking the relations of the sacred and the profane, perhaps also of the real and the unreal, of the one and the many. This is about as much as Yeats would claim. At another door, Auden's anti-mythological attitude would seem to be a myth of its own, a belittlement of traditional glories only to make a reduced but very solid residual claim, like stripping a Victorian house of its gingerbread in order to display its solidity.

At least once in later poems Yeats and Auden converge on the same subject. This is a moment of lay sanctity experienced in a restaurant. Auden is full of casual and seemingly gratuitous detail:

In Schrafft's

Having finished the Blue-plate Special
And reached the coffee stage,
Stirring her cup she sat,
A somewhat shapeless figure
Of indeterminate age
In an undistinguished hat.

When she lifted her eyes it was plain
That our globular future,
Our international rout
Of sin and apparatus

> And dying men galore,
> Was not being bothered about.
>
> Which of the seven heavens
> Was responsible her smile
> Wouldn't be sure but attested
> That, whoever it was, a god
> Worth kneeling-to for a while
> Had tabernacled and rested.

Yeats's poem on a similar theme comes in the series called 'Vacillation':

> My fiftieth year had come and gone,
> I sat, a solitary man,
> In a crowded London shop,
> An open book and empty cup
> On the marble table-top.
>
> While on the shop and street I gazed
> My body of a sudden blazed;
> And twenty minutes more or less
> It seemed, so great my happiness,
> That I was blessèd and could bless.

Auden carries the commonplaceness of the shop a little further than Yeats, and he limits the intensity of the experience described. Characteristically the latter is not his own, but that of someone 'shapeless' he doesn't know, of indeterminate age, who wears an undistinguished hat, as if she were describable only in negative terms. The religious imagery is operated differently in the two poems: it serves Yeats to describe a blasphemous encroachment of the human upon the divine, while in Auden an earthier god makes his positive incursion upon the human, an incursion less weighty, less implicating, more sanguine. Auden's metaphor is genuinely religious and yet ironically reduced: food in the tabernacle of the belly constitutes a certain good.

The movement has been from candid intensity to intense

candor. Auden's offhand, unassuming tone, his disinfected vocabulary, take on some of their authority by disavowing what in
Yeats is so assuming, so infected. As Proust remarks, 'A powerful
idea communicates some of its strength to him who challenges
it.' If Yeats, and poets like him, had not already extolled the
poem as a terrestrial paradise, a fragment of Eden, a symbol of
heaven, Auden might have felt less disposed to belittle it as a
'verbal contraption.' These terms are not mutually exclusive:
they represent different kinds of assertion and defiance at different moments. Yeats with overstatement, and Auden with understatement, circle furtively toward each other, caught in the same
galactic system.

Notes

THE numerals at the left refer to page numbers in this book. The words that follow the numerals indicate the beginning and end of the phrase or passage that is being annotated.

I. Introduction

7. Come, heart, where hill ... his lonely horn, / Yeats, 'Into the Twilight.'
   This and other ...—supper is spread, / Yeats, *The Land of Heart's Desire*, in *The Variorum Edition of the Plays of W. B. Yeats*, ed. Russell K. Alspach (New York, 1966), p. 183.

8. I told him: ... man alone of noon, / John Berryman, 'The Animal Trainer (1).'
   Though he says boldly, ... a man named Yeats,' / Theodore Roethke, 'The Dance' in 'Four for Sir John Davies.'

II. Oscar and Oisin

9. 'To an Irishman,' ... 'England is fairyland.' / R. Ellmann, *Yeats: The Man and the Masks* (New York, 1948), p. 76.

9-10. When Hugh Kingsmill ... the nobles of Baghdad. / Hesketh Pearson, *The Life of Oscar Wilde* (London, 1946), p. 169.

10. Yeats could not deny ... consider him 'cold-blooded,' / Yeats, 'Oscar Wilde's Last Book,' *United Ireland* (26 September 1891), 5.

10. 'To Shaw, ... his Rosicrucian fans.' / Bernard Shaw, letter to R. Ellmann, 17 October 1946.

In his *Autobiography* ... praised it without qualification. / W. B. Yeats, *Autobiography* (New York, 1965), pp. 89–90.

10–11. His sense of Wilde's generosity ... devoted to the book. / Wilde's two reviews were 'Some Literary Notes,' *Woman's World* II:17 (March 1889) 277–80, and 'Three New Poets,' *Pall Mall Gazette* XLIX:7587 (12 July 1889) 3.

11. They were grounded on ... English romanticism. / Wilde, 'The English Renaissance of Art,' *passim*.

12. On 25 July 1888 ... 'My Irish Poet.' / Letter to Katharine Tynan, 25 July 1888, in Yeats, *Letters of W. B. Yeats*, ed. Allan Wade (London, 1954), p. 80.

This praise was filially quoted ... as well. / Wilde, 'Some Literary Notes,' *Woman's World* II:16 (February 1889) 221–24.

In his *Autobiography* ... William Ernest Henley's. / Yeats, *Autobiography*, pp. 87–8.

and when Yeats referred ... talker of our time.' / Yeats, 'Lady Wilde,' *Boston Pilot*, 28 September 1889, in *Letters to the New Island*, ed. Horace Reynolds (Cambridge, Massachusetts, 1934), p. 77.

12–13. He voiced something ... invent his own myth.' / Yeats, unpublished first draft of *Autobiography*.

13. Much of his work ... all he did and thought.' / Yeats, 'At Stratford-on-Avon,' May 1901, in *Essays and Introductions* (London, 1961), p. 107.

The sense of living ... to conceive of himself.' / John Eglinton [W. K. Magee], A *Memoir of AE, George William Russell* (London, 1937), pp. 110–11.

'But,' someone ... in either world.' / Yeats, *Autobiography*, p. 87.

He did in fact ... an excellent talker. / Wilde, 'The Critic as Artist,' and Yeats, 'An Excellent Talker' [review of *A Woman of No Importance*], *Bookman* (March 1895), 182.

14. 'Overshadowed by old men ... Victorian fault.' / Yeats,

'Introduction' to *Oxford Book of Modern Verse* (Oxford, 1936), pp. vi–vii.

14. 'He thought he was ... to be a poet.' / Yeats, letter to Sturge Moore, 6 May 1906, in W. B. Yeats and T. Sturge Moore, *Their Correspondence*, ed. Ursula Bridge (London, 1953), pp. 8–9.

Something of this verdict ... talkers since the Greeks.' / Yeats, *Autobiography*, p. 90.

17. Yeats pursued ... Buddha's emptiness.' / Yeats, 'The Statues.'

'Think of what we owe ... imitation of Caesar.' / Slightly misquoted in Yeats, *Autobiography*, p. 181.

Some years ago ... meditation upon a mask. / Yeats, *Per Amica Silentia Lunae* (1917) in *Mythologies* (New York, 1959), pp. 333–34.

18. Queens that have laughed ... what it choose. / Yeats, letter to J. B. Yeats, 7 August 1909, in Yeats, *Letters*, p. 534. Wade printed 'And those' for 'But those.'

'The nineteenth century ... of Balzac.' / Wilde, 'The Decay of Lying.'

18–19. In a sentence ... Lucien de Rubempré.' / Ibid.

19. Yeats cavilled at ... object to the content. / Yeats, *Autobiography*, p. 90.

Corot's paintings ... Renoir's images of them. / Marcel Proust, *The Guermantes Way*, Part II (New York, 1933), pp. 21–22.

19–20. As he writes ... its goal, its fixed type.' / Yeats, *On the Boiler* (Dublin, [1939]), p. 37. Wilde, in turn, had borrowed the idea from Pater's essay on Winckelmann, itself somewhat indebted to Hegel.

21. 'The beryl stone ... outside the window.' / Yeats, 'The Symbolism of Poetry,' 1900, in *Essays and Introductions*, p. 163.

He did, however, dwell ... of physical energy.' / Wilde, *De Profundis*, in *The Works of Oscar Wilde*, ed. G. F. Maine (London, 1948), p. 884.

22. Love's pleasure ... consumes his dreams, / Yeats, 'Two Songs from a Play.'

22. One day Wilde said . . . Christian heresy.   /   Yeats, *Auto-biography*, p. 91.

Another fable, . . . 'terrible beauty.'   /   Ibid., p. 190.

23. There was much . . . lacking in tension.   /   Yeats, letter to Sturge Moore, in Yeats and Moore, *Their Correspondence*, pp 8–9.

23–4. He went reluctantly . . . the sainted author.'   /   Yeats, unpublished letter to John Quinn, 30 May 1905.

24. On the other hand, . . . a part of our time,   /   Letter to René Francis, 5 September 1911, in Yeats, *Letters*, p. 562.

He replaced the atmosphere . . . risen god.'   /   Letter to Mrs. Olivia Shakespear, 7 August 1934, in Yeats, *Letters*, p. 826.

'Even when disaster struck him down . . . clear his soul.'   /   'Introduction' to *Oxford Book of Modern Verse*, p. vii.

Though on release . . . heart was shallow.'   /   Yeats, unpublished first draft of *Autobiography*.

24–5. Yeats summed it up . . . sketch of a great man.'   /   A note dated 1904, written by Yeats in John Quinn's copy of *The Land of Heart's Desire*, published in Allan Wade, *A Bibliography of the Writings of W. B. Yeats* (London, 1958), p. 30.

25. The 'good things' . . .   /   A phrase used in Yeats's letter to Katharine Tynan, 27 February 1890, *Letters*, p. 151.

What was best . . . rake or gambler,   /   Yeats, 'Oscar Wilde's Last Book,' *United Ireland* (26 September 1891) 5.

or to 'an audacious . . . figure.'   /   Yeats, *Autobiography*, p. 87.

Symons spoke of decadence . . . ideal of Decadence.'   /   Arthur Symons, 'The Decadent Movement in Literature,' November 1893, in *Aesthetes and Decadents of the 1890s*, ed. Karl Beckson (New York, 1966), p. 141.

In 1898 he declared . . . autumn of the flesh.'   /   Yeats, 'The Autumn of the Flesh,' *Daily Express* (Dublin), 3 December 1898.

27. Stevens . . . the reflection of literature.'   /   Wallace Stevens, *Opus Posthumous* (New York, 1957), p. 159.

III. *The Hawklike Man*

29. It is the gregarious ... longs for 'a place of stone' /
   Yeats, 'To a Friend Whose Work Has Come to Nothing.'
30. In *The Celtic Twilight* ... 'delicate scepticism,' / Joyce,
   'The Soul of Ireland' (26 March 1903), in *Critical
   Writings*, ed. Ellsworth Mason and Richard Ellmann
   (New York, 1959), p. 104.
32. Bend down your faces ... the loud waters, / A *Portrait
   of the Artist as a Young Man* (New York, 1964), p. 225.
   He has Bloom overhear ... could happen him....' /
   Ulysses (New York, 1961), p. 609.
33. 'What Morals, if any, ... Diarmuid and Grania?' / *Finnegans Wake* (New York, 1939), p. 307.
34. Frank Fay attempted ... English-speaking populace. /
   Fay's review is reprinted in *The Workshop of Dedalus*,
   ed. Robert Scholes and Richard M. Kain (Evanston, Illinois, 1965), pp. 158–9.
   In 'The Day ... Irish dramatists in turn. / This essay is
   given in *Critical Writings*, pp. 68–72.
   Yeats gave no indication ... one learns nothing.' / Letter from Yeats to Joyce, October 1902, in *Letters of
   James Joyce*, Vol. II, ed. Richard Ellmann (London and
   New York, 1966), p. 14.
   Long afterwards, ... poetry of onanism.' / Conversation
   with Clarke, 1947.
   Probably he had ... inside a 'beehut.' / *Finnegans
   Wake*, pp. 605–606.
35. 'To me an Irish ... English epic.' / Ellmann, *James
   Joyce* (New York and London, 1959), p. 436.
36. Yet, if the evidence ... planes of consciousness.' / *Ulysses*, p. 140.
   The subject was ... the method of *Ulysses* / *Letters of
   Joyce*, Vol. III, p. 83.
   but since James ... 'incapable of any belief' / *Letters
   of Joyce*, Vol. II, p. 89.
36–7. He next communicated ... self-confidence rather interesting.' / Letter from Russell to Yeats, ?11 August 1902,

in *Letters from AE*, ed. Alan Denson (London and New York, 1961), p. 43.

37. In a middle-aged disclaimer . . . younger had no part.' / Gorman papers, University of Southern Illinois Library. What this means . . . too worm and early.' / *Finnegans Wake*, p. 37.

39. As he phrased the problem . . . mixed it and so few modern. . . .' / Yeats, 'Preface' to *The Unicorn from the Stars and Other Plays* (New York, 1908). To all this . . . a man of letters.' / Yeats, *Autobiography*, pp. 111–12.

40. In Nighttown . . . O good God, take him!' / *Ulysses*, p. 600; cf. p. 595. Yeats, left alone . . . Oxford literary set.' / Letter from Yeats to Joyce, in *Letters of Joyce*, Vol. II, p. 13. On his way to . . . for 'a motive' / Letter to Stanislaus Joyce, 8 February 1903, in *Letters of Joyce*, Vol. II, p. 28.

41. He found Joyce . . . Ibsenite fury.' / Yeats, *Letters*, p. 386. From Paris Joyce sent . . . for submission. / Letter from Yeats to Joyce, 18 December 1902, in *Letters of Joyce*, Vol. II, p. 23. The folk plays . . . as 'dwarf-dramas.' / Joyce, 'The Soul of Ireland,' in *Critical Writings*, pp. 103–104. Applying the principles . . . beginning to end. / *Letters of Joyce*, Vol. II, pp. 212, 35, 38.

41–2. —Longworth is awfully . . . thinks of Homer. / *Ulysses*, p. 216.

42. Yeats met him . . . unexpectedly well.' / Yeats, *Letters*, p. 399.

44. Yeats returned the plays . . . send him money. / *Letters of Joyce*, Vol. II, p. 58. O, hold me still . . . heavy hair, / Joyce, *Stephen Hero*, ed. Theodore Spencer (Norfolk, Connecticut, 1963), p. 37.

45–6. One day an officer . . . that followed it. / Ibid., pp. 242–43. These additional pages have been edited by John J. Slocum and Herbert Cahoon.

46. John Alphonsus . . . mean him no harm. / A *Portrait,* pp. 251–52.

47. On one visit . . . 'The Holy Office.' / *Letters of Joyce,* Vol. II, p. 298.
    In despair at . . . literature of our country.' / Ibid., p. 322.

48. He was not given . . . were anything but routine. / Ibid., p. 354.
    Of *Chamber Music* . . . symbolical theme. / Ibid., pp. 354, 351, 356.
    Of *Dubliners* Yeats . . . of a new kind.' / Ibid., pp. 356, 354.
    Having read some . . . talent in Ireland today.' / Ibid., p. 356.
    A little later . . . 'a very great book.' / Ibid., p. 388.
    Before reading it . . . a riot for it.' / Ibid.
    But after reading . . . forward to reading that. / Ibid., p. 405.

49. I am making . . . novelist of our time. / Yeats, *Letters,* p. 651.
    As he wrote Mrs. Olivia . . . pleasure to shoot him.' / Ibid., p. 679.
    Two months later . . . Barsetshire novels alternately. / Ibid., p. 682.

49–50. Late in 1922 . . . be remembered to Yeats. / Unpublished letter, 9 August 1922.

50. 'If he comes,' . . . of men of letters.' / Yeats, *Letters,* p. 698.
    The invitation was renewed . . . politely declined. / *Letters of Joyce,* Vol. III, p. 100.

50–51. In them 'there is hatred . . . pursue and terrify.' / Yeats, *A Vision* (London, 1925—actually 1926), pp. 211–12. To avoid confusion I have left out some ellipses.

52. 'One thinks of Joyce's . . . of his own mind.' / Yeats, 'Bishop Berkeley,' in *Essays and Introductions,* p. 405.

53. Joyce went on citing . . . that for imagination.' / Eugene Jolas, 'My Friend James Joyce,' in *James Joyce: Two Decades of Criticism,* ed. Seon Givens (New York, 1948), pp. 14–15.

53. In June 1935 he ... he is such a fool!' / Letter to
George Joyce, 25 June 1935, in *Letters of Joyce*, Vol. I,
ed. Stuart Gilbert (New York, 1957), pp. 371–72.
'We feel ... that it is ... the death of Synge.' / Article
in the *Irish Times*, 11 August 1924. See also *Letters of
Joyce*, Vol. I, p. 220.
'I am not going to defend ... of an heroic mind.' / *The
Senate Speeches of W. B. Yeats*, ed. Donald R. Pearce
(London, 1961), pp. 147–48.

54. 'Of course the first name ... an empty sack indeed.' /
Included in *Letters of Joyce*, Vol. III, pp. 258–59.
'It is now thirty years ... good enough to send me.' /
Letters of Joyce, Vol. I, p. 325.
Joyce said he preferred ... envisioned by John. / Joyce,
'Daniel Defoe,' ed. Joseph Prescott, *Buffalo Studies* I
(December 1964), 25.

55–6. As he said of Stephen ... were as one to him, / Joyce,
A Portrait, p. 168.

IV. *Ez and Old Billyum*

57. Instead he declared, ... worthy of serious study, / Ezra
Pound, 'Status Rerum,' *Poetry* I.4 (January 1913) 123.
and in later years ... how Yeats did it.' / Letter to
Michael Roberts, July 1937, in *The Letters of Ezra
Pound*, ed. D. D. Paige (New York, 1950), p. 296.
What he learned ... containing an image,' / Pound,
'Harold Monro,' in *Polite Essays* (London, 1937), p. 9.
Although you hide ... the moon is set, / Pound, 'The
Later Yeats,' *Poetry* IX.3 (December 1917) 65–66.
the inner form of the line, / Pound, 'On Music,' *New
Age* X.15 (8 February 1912) 343–44.
probably its ... 'dull, numb words' / Yeats, *Dramatis
Personae* (London, 1936), p. 53.
Yeats offered further ... 'syntactical simplicity'; / Pound,
'This Hulme Business,' *Townsman* II.5 (January 1939)
15.

57–8. he had, for example, ... 'Everything alters.' / Pound,
'The Later Yeats,' *Poetry* IX.3 (December 1917) 66.

58. Fergus, who abdicated . . . in the forest, / Yeats, 'Who Goes with Fergus?'
    'They will not hush, . . . beech leaves old.' / The wording of this line was changed somewhat later.
59. Miraut has been patched . . . fourth volumes of verse, / 'The Madness of King Goll' is from *The Wanderings of Oisin and Other Poems* (1889); 'He Thinks of His Past Greatness . . .' from *The Wind Among the Reeds* (1899); and 'In the Seven Woods' from the volume of the same name (1904).
60. When he read . . . knew to be reserved. / Pound, letter to William Carlos Williams, 21 October 1908, in *Letters*, p. 4.
    The title proudly . . . series of exotic roles. / Ibid., pp. 3–4.
61. and Pound wrote elatedly . . . greatest living poet.' / Pound, letter to Williams, 21 May 1909, in *Letters*, pp. 7–8.
    In December 1909, . . . on the troubadours.' / Yeats, letter to Lady Gregory, 10 December 1909, in Yeats, *Letters*, p. 543.
    So much erudition . . . British Museum. / Pound, letter to Sarah Perkins Cope, 22 April 1934, in *Letters*, p. 257.
    But he noted also . . . on a bad phonograph.' / Yeats, letter to Lady Gregory, 10 December 1909, in Yeats, *Letters*, p. 543.
    Pound, for his part, . . . *The Wind Among the Reeds*. / Pound, letter to Felix E. Schelling, 8 July 1922, in *Letters*, p. 180.
62. As John Butler Yeats . . . with the Furies.' / Letter from J. B. Yeats to W. B. Yeats, 12 March 1918, in J. B. Yeats, *Letters to His Son W. B. Yeats and Others*, ed. Joseph Hone (New York, 1946), pp. 244–45.
    by his rule, Yeats . . . dry and clear. / A. R. Jones, *The Life and Opinions of Thomas Ernest Hulme* (London, 1960), pp. 29–31.
    T. S. Eliot, . . . in the modern world. / T. S. Eliot, 'A Foreign Mind,' [review of Yeats's *The Cutting of an Agate*] *Athenaeum* 4653 (4 July 1919) 552–53.

62. By 1912 D. H. Lawrence . . . wouldn't bear touching, /
Lawrence, letter to A. W. McLeod, 17 December 1912,
in *The Collected Letters of D. H. Lawrence*, ed. Harry
T. Moore (New York, 1962), Vol. I, p. 168.

and he objected . . . as 'sickly.' / Lawrence, letter to
Gordon Campbell, 19 December 1914, ibid., p. 302.

Another friend of Pound's, . . . but a gargoyle.' / Pound,
'This Hulme Business,' *Townsman* II.5 (January 1939)
15.

62-3. The magistrate was . . . many of its faults.' / Pound,
'Status Rerum,' *Poetry* I.4 (January 1913) 123-27.

63. In 1913 Pound wrote . . . set in the past.' / Pound, letter to Harriet Monroe, 13 August 1913, in *Letters*, p. 21.

Such reservations did not . . . and the symbolists, /
Pound, letter to René Taupin, May 1928, in *Letters*, p.
218.

These movements, . . . view of the verse line. / 'And
now one has got with the camera an *enormous* correlation
of particulars. That capacity for making contact is a tre-
mendous challenge to literature.' Pound quoted in *Writers at Work* (Second Series) (New York, 1963), p. 41.

Tagore's poetry brought together . . . fastidious with the
popular / Yeats, 'Introduction' to Rabindranath
Tagore, *Gitanjali* (New York, 1916), pp. xiii–xv.

Yeats remarked to Pound, . . . trying to write.' / Pound,
letter to Harriet Monroe, October 1912, in Harriet Monroe, *A Poet's Life* (New York, 1938), p. 262. Cf. Pound,
'Rabindranath Tagore,' *Fortnightly Review* XCIII
(N.S.).555 (1 March 1913) 571–79.

63-4. Pointing to a . . . not out of literature.' / Pound,
'French Poets,' in *Make It New* (New Haven, 1935),
p. 245.

64. His friend Sturge Moore . . . about words. / W. B. Yeats
and T. Sturge Moore, *Their Correspondence*, pp. 22,
190.

he insisted upon the word 'girl.') / Yeats, letter to Dorothy Wellesley, 21 December 1935, in Yeats, *Letters*,
p. 846.

Soon he recognized . . . mainly 'great beauty,' / Yeats,

letter to Edmund Gosse, 25 November 1912, in ibid., pp. 572–73.

64. The note was bound, ... atmosphere of drama.' / Pound, unpublished letter to Harriet Monroe, 4 November 1912, in the University of Chicago Library.

64–5. At peace, he sent ... the new phase.' / Pound, letter to Harriet Monroe, 26 October 1912, in the University of Chicago Library. It is slightly misquoted in Monroe, *A Poet's Life*, p. 264.

65. Pound, though he ... 'No Second Troy,' / Pound, 'The Later Yeats,' *Poetry* IX.3 (December 1917) 66.

On November 2, ... le roi désire!' / Pound, unpublished letter to Harriet Monroe, 2 November 1912, in the University of Chicago Library.

Final clinic ... reigns on parnassus. / Pound, letter to Harriet Monroe, also 2 November 1912, but sent separately from above letter, in the University of Chicago Library.

65–6. It was probably now ... merely set up another.' / Pound, 'French Poets,' *Make It New*, p. 245.

66. In the former he writes: ... Miltonic generalizations.' / Yeats, letter to Lady Gregory, 1 January 1913, in 'Some New Letters from W. B. Yeats to Lady Gregory,' ed. Donald T. Torchiana and Glenn O'Malley, *Review of English Literature* IV.3 (July 1963) 14.

He was later ... 'conventional metaphors,' / Yeats, 'A General Introduction for My Work,' in *Essays and Introductions* (London, 1961), p. 525.

My digestion has got ... principles than taste. / Yeats, letter to Lady Gregory, 3 January 1913, quoted in A. N. Jeffares, *W. B. Yeats: Man and Poet* (New Haven, 1949), p. 167.

66–7. In terms ostentatiously ... sense of your sincerity.' / Pound, letter to Harriet Monroe, in *Letters*, p. 49.

67. For him, as for Auden later, / W. H. Auden, *The Dyer's Hand* (New York, 1962), p. 50.

He showed Pound ... a review of *Responsibilities*) / Pound, 'The Later Yeats,' p. 67.

67. But he was nonetheless ... become a modern poet. /
    Interview with Mrs. W. B. Yeats, 1946.
68. He quarreled with ... 'devil's metres.' / Pound, 'The
    Later Yeats,' p. 65.
    'I suggest him to you ... orthodoxy not inspired.' /
    Yeats, letter to Harriet Monroe, ?December 1913, in
    Monroe, *A Poet's Life*, pp. 330–31.
    The latter he complimented, ... real organic rhythm.' /
    Yeats, speech given in March 1914, ibid., p. 338.
    He quoted it again later in A *Vision*, / Yeats, A *Vision*
    (New York, 1938), pp. 29–30.
    'The antipodes of ... vigorous saliency.' / Pound, un-
    published letter to Harriet Monroe, 24 December 1915,
    from Stone Cottage, in the University of Chicago
    Library.
69. He had formed ... companion in mind, / Yeats, letter
    to J. B. Yeats, 5 August 1913, in Yeats, *Letters*, p. 584.
    He expected that ... bore him. / Pound, letter to Isabel
    Pound, November 1913, in *Letters*, p. 25.
    He wrote Williams ... midst of the whirl.' / Pound,
    letter to Williams, 19 December 1913, in *Letters*, p. 27.
70. In the edition ... furnished him by Yeats, / Ernest
    Fenollosa and Ezra Pound, '*Noh*' or *Accomplishment*
    (London, 1916), pp. 27, 44, 91, 106.
    and speaks with ... hypnotizeability of ghosts,' / Ibid.,
    p. 31. Pound was himself prompted to read in occult
    literature, notably in John Heydon, first mentioned in
    the discarded Canto III and later in *Guide to Kulchur*,
    p. 225. While in St. Elizabeth's Hospital, Pound bor-
    rowed the book again from Mrs. Yeats, and he quotes
    directly from it in Canto XCI.
    only the merit ... to this pass. / Fenollosa and Pound,
    '*Noh*' or *Accomplishment*, p. 44.
71. The Samurai are ... Kiltartan or Aran: / A point noted
    by T. S. Eliot in his review, 'The Noh and the Image,'
    Egoist IV.7 (August 1917) 102–103.
    I've a sad heart ... wild, desolate place? / Fenollosa and
    Pound, '*Noh*' or *Accomplishment*, p. 30.

71. Times out of mind . . . in this mountain.   /   Ibid., p. 132.
I had my own . . . night, surely.   /   Ibid., p. 33.
The Noh plays were . . . them as a failure.   /   Pound,
letter to John Quinn, 4 June 1918, in *Letters*, p. 137.
He linked them . . . *Silentia Lunae*,   /   Ibid.
though his allusion . . . 'Willie' (for 'Ille')   /   Interview
with Mrs. W. B. Yeats, 1946.
He was prepared . . . Yeats was 'faded.'   /   Pound, letter
to Williams, 11 September 1920, in *Letters*, p. 158.

72. Yeats saw how . . . on a single metaphor.   /   Yeats, 'Certain Noble Plays of Japan,' in *Essays and Introductions*,
p. 234.
He offered many . . . scenery and timing;   /   Two letters
from Pound to Yeats, in Mrs. Yeats's possession, deal
with the problems of staging the play. One has several
sketches included.
He wrote a skit . . . full of indecencies.   /   Pound, letter
to Iris Barry, September 1916, in *Letters*, p. 96.
Then Yeats recommended . . . also was vetoed.   /   Yeats,
unpublished letter to Lady Gregory, 21 June 1916, in
Mrs. Yeats's possession. Pound had made clear he would
not come as permanent manager.

73. He wote a poem, . . . 'a little bad Yeats'),   /   Pound, letter to Harriet Monroe, 17 May 1915, in *Letters*, p. 60.
Pound saw her . . . other to Maud Gonne.   /   Pound, letter to John Quinn, 15 November 1918, in *Letters*, p.
140; Yeats, letter to Lady Gregory, 1 April 1928, in Yeats,
Letters, p. 738.

73–4. Pound wrote the criticism . . . repeating it.   /   Pound,
letter to Kate Buss, 9 March 1916, in *Letters*, p. 72.
Yeats was quoting a sentence of Tulka which he used as
an epigraph to *Early Poems and Stories* (1925): 'Give
me the world if thou wilt, but grant me an asylum for
my affections.'

74. He told Pound . . . liked *Mauberley*,   /   Pound, unpublished letter to Homer Pound, 1 September 1920, quoted
by Thomas Parkinson, 'Yeats and Pound: The Illusion
of Influence,' *Comparative Literature* VI (Summer
1954) 256–64.

74. and he tried ... about the *Cantos*. / Yeats, 'Introduction' to *Oxford Book of Modern Verse*, p. xxv.

(Yeats speaks elsewhere ... it as successful.) / Yeats, Journal kept in January 1929, quoted by Ellmann, *The Identity of Yeats* (New York, 1964), p. 239.

He is thereby enabled ... object of desire. / Yeats, *A Vision* (1938), p. 128.

75. It loathes abstraction ... sound and metaphor. / Ibid., p. 127.

Unable to discover ... self-conscious poses. / Ibid.

'One says "I am" ... more elaborate masks.' / Pound, *Gaudier-Brzeska* (London, 1916), p. 98.

More by chance ... sword of the swashbuckler.' / *A Vision* (1938), p. 128.

He oscillates between ... have lasting value. / Ibid.

76. This undifferentiated pity, ... romantic movement. / *A Vision* (1938), p. 6.

He had observed ... and Wilfred Owen. / Yeats quarreled with O'Casey over *The Silver Tassie* on this account; his comments on Owen are in Yeats, *Letters*, pp. 874–75.

Instead of allowing ... the world boil over. / *A Vision* (1938), pp. 128, 166.

Not only is ... sequence being knowable, / Ellmann, *Identity of Yeats*, p. 239.

'There is no transmission ... without movement.' / Yeats, 'Introduction' to *Oxford Book of Modern Verse*, p. xxiv.

He found an Eastern ... pulpited and bewigged), / Yeats, letter to Lady Gregory, 7 April 1930, in Yeats, *Letters*, p. 774.

but in Sankara, ... the waves themselves.' / Yeats, 'Preface' to *Fighting the Waves*, in *Explorations* (London, 1962), p. 373. He was alluding to Stendhal's image of the novel as a 'mirror moving along a highway.'

76–7. The new literature ... of authorship. / Yeats, *A Vision* (1938), pp. 299–300, 165; 'Pages from a Diary Written in 1930,' in *Explorations*, p. 294.

77. In a letter ... did *not* contain, / Yeats, unpublished

letter to Harriet Monroe, 8 February 1931, in the University of Chicago Library.

77. Because of this submission . . . like a theologian. / Yeats, *A Vision* (1925), pp. 210–11.

By holding apart . . . a mechanical force. / Yeats, *A Vision* (1925), p. 213.

78. Overcome, O bitter . . . loveless dust. / In Mrs. W. B. Yeats's possession. Ellmann, *Identity of Yeats*, pp. 131–32.

Acting on this impulse, . . . opposite of mine.' / Yeats, *A Vision* (1938), p. 3.

78–9. He summarized . . . keep Pound neighborly. / Yeats, letter to Lady Gregory, 1 April 1928, in Yeats, *Letters*, p. 739.

79. He did his best, . . . had become a shibboleth. / Yeats, *A Vision* (1938), pp. 4–5; 'Introduction' to *Oxford Book of Modern Verse*, p. xxiv.

Yeats also included . . . retain moral ascendancy.' / Yeats, *A Vision* (1938), p. 26; cf. 'Preface' to *The Senate Speeches of W. B. Yeats*, ed. Donald R. Pearce, p. 25.

Vex not thou . . . save to the blind. / Reprinted in *Personae* (New York, new edition, no date), p. 263.

79–80. Yeats wrote there: . . . everything in the symbol.' / Yeats, *A Vision* (1938), p. 301.

80. Contrary to Yeats, . . . mermaids, that carving / Cf. Hugh Kenner, *The Poetry of Ezra Pound* (London, 1951), p. 210, and Donald Davie, *Ezra Pound: Poet as Sculptor* (New York, 1964), pp. 180–81. As Davie notes, *Les Paradis artificiels* is Baudelaire's book about drugs. But the primary allusion would seem to be to Yeats's poem.

and he repeats . . . the latter church. / Canto LXXIV, p. 8; Canto LXXVI, p. 38.

81. In recounting . . . to be reliable. / Yeats, 'Preface' to *The King of the Great Clock Tower* (New York, 1934).

In his notebook . . . prose to get structure.' / Unpublished notebook of Yeats, begun at Rapallo in June 1934.

82. He also let Pound know, . . . at the Abbey. / Yeats,

letter to Mrs. Olivia Shakespear, 7 August 1934, in Yeats, *Letters*, pp. 826–27.

82. In another letter ... the buzzard.' / Quoted by Thomas Parkinson, 'Yeats and Pound: The Illusion of Influence,' p. 263.

But at the last meeting ... recent poems, / Parkinson, *W. B. Yeats: The Later Poetry* (Berkeley and Los Angeles, 1964), p. 177.

83. As he thought ... for all his violence.' / Yeats, letter to Dorothy Wellesley, 8 September 1935, in *Letters on Poetry from W. B. Yeats to Dorothy Wellesley* (New York, 1940), p. 25.

In the preface he said ... stammering confusion.' / Yeats, 'Introduction' to *Oxford Book of Modern Verse*, p. xxv.

The trait of nobility ... in 1916; / Pound in 'The Later Yeats,' p. 67, speaks of 'a curious nobility, a nobility which is, to me at least, the very core of Mr. Yeats' production, the constant element of his writing.'

Not having achieved ... wine into the bowl. / Yeats, 'Introduction' to *Oxford Book of Modern Verse*, p. xxvi.

Pound did not respond ... to stand on.' / Canto 98, p. 37; Canto 102, p. 80.

When in 1917 ... its thoughts in.' / Pound, Canto I, *Poetry* X.3 (June 1917) 113, 115.

After having read and ... never getting an outline.' / Pound, letter to Eliot, 24 December 1921, in *Letters*, p. 169.

84. but the beauty ... make it cohere. / Quoted by Donald Davie, *Times Literary Supplement* (25 May 1967) 472.

The Japanese professor ... and the imaginative.' / Shotaro Oshima, *W. B. Yeats and Japan* (Tokyo, 1965), p. 104.

85. as he insisted to Stephen Spender, ... tapestrylike, / Spender, *World within World* (London, 1951), p. 164.

The two poets were ... of the mind,' / Pound quoted in *Writers at Work*, p. 56.

86. 'UBI AMOR IBI OCULUS EST,' / Canto 90, p. 69.

or as he says . . . dove sta memoria. . . .   /   Canto LXXVI,
p. 35; cf. Canto LXXVII, p. 44.

86. The two positions . . . for him to work with;   /   Pound
quoted in *Writers at Work*, pp. 41–42.

'beastly and cantankerous' for Pound,'   /   Pound, Canto
I (later completely revised), *Poetry* X.3 (June 1917) 115.

'half dead at the top' for Yeats.   /   Yeats, 'Blood and the
Moon.'

('My dear William . . . *Cantos* admonished.)   /   Canto
LXXIX, p. 65.

For Yeats the cure . . . arrange experience.   /   Yeats, *A
Vision* (1938), p. 25.

Pound thought . . . of particulars.'   /   Canto LXXIV, p.
19.

Pound's view . . . 'improvisatory,'   /   Yeats, 'Introduction'
to *Oxford Book of Modern Verse*, p. xxvi.

V. *Possum's Conversion*

89. For Eliot as a young . . . a protracted Pre-Raphaelite, . . .   /
Eliot, 'Yeats,' *On Poetry and Poets* (London, 1957),
p. 256.

while for Yeats . . . poetry resemble prose.   /   Yeats, 'Introduction' to *Oxford Book of Modern Verse*, pp. xxi–
xxiii.

To others as well . . . flat, bare.   /   Ibid. Cf. 'Modern
Poetry,' in *Essays and Introductions*, pp. 499–500, and
letter to Dorothy Wellesley, 21 December 1935, in
Letters on Poetry, p. 48.

90. At his most indulgent, . . . older or newer thought.'   /
Yeats, 'Preface' to *The Ten Principal Upanishads*, trans-
lated by Shree Purohit Swami and W. B. Yeats (New
York, 1937), p. 10.

Yeats thought he saw . . . instead of one.   /   See the passage from *A Vision* (1925), on pp. 50–51 above.

Yeats's two subjects . . . Moore and spooks.'   /   Interview
with Eliot, 1947.

Once he hit on 1916, . . . its diction.   /   Interview with
Eliot, 1947.

90–91. His surprise was . . . modern verse drama. / 'Poetry and Drama,' *On Poetry and Poets*, p. 78.

Nineteen-nineteen is . . . won over to Yeats, / Eliot, 'Yeats,' *On Poetry and Poets*, p. 252.

But this date . . . to escape from.' / Eliot, 'A Foreign Mind,' *Athenaeum* 4653 (4 July 1919) 552–53.

'His remoteness . . . world to escape from.' / Ibid.

Miss Weston has little . . . basis of magical practices. / Jessie L. Weston, *From Ritual to Romance* (New York, 1957), pp. 79, 98.

92. In 1923, reviewing *Ulysses*, . . . antiquity. / Eliot, 'Ulysses, Order, and Myth,' *Dial* LXXV.5 (November 1923) 480–83.

Evidently Eliot . . . Yeats or Hardy.' / Pound, letter to H. L. Mencken, February 1925, in *Letters*, p. 198.

There is some confirmation . . . *Strange Gods*. / Eliot, *After Strange Gods* (New York, 1933), pp. 48–51.

93. And Eliot concludes . . . greatest odds.' / Ibid.

He devoted a leading . . . late diction. / Eliot, 'A Commentary,' *Criterion* XIV.57 (July 1935) 610–13.

In the 'provincial' . . . in any language.' / Eliot, 'The Poetry of W. B. Yeats,' *Southern Review* VII.3 (Winter 1941) 442.

He later omitted . . . an obituary. / See 'Yeats' in *On Poetry and Poets*.

94. Though not named, . . . Yeats and Swift, / Eliot so informed Professor Kristian Smidt.

VI. *Gazebos and Gashouses*

98. As Auden observes . . . Social Concern, / W. H. Auden, 'Yeats: Master of Diction,' a review of *Last Poems*, *Saturday Review of Literature* XXII:7 (8 June 1940) 14.

98–9. We can detect . . . and—despaired; / T. S. Eliot, *The Waste Land*, III, line 190.

99. Auden pushed past . . . large turbine?' / Auden, 'The Engine House,' in Christopher Isherwood, *Lions and Shadows* (Norfolk, Connecticut, 1947), p. 186.

much as Hart Crane . . . and exulted; / Hart Crane, 'The River,' in *The Bridge* (1930).

99. Just as in 1900, . . . outmoded scientific epoch,   /   Yeats,
    letter to Lady Gregory, 12 March 1900, in *Letters*, p.
    335.
    so he was capable . . . submission to it.   /   Yeats, 'Modern
    Poetry,' in *Essays and Introductions* (London, 1961),
    p. 499; see also his description of phases 23 and 24 in
    A Vision.
100. Cheer up! . . . Parnell's heart.   /   Auden and Louis Mac-
    Neice, *Letters from Iceland* (London, 1937), p. 233.
    The allusion to . . . metaphor of Eliot,   /   Eliot, 'Ash
    Wednesday' (1930), I.
    In a little poem . . . Parnell's heart,   /   Yeats, 'Parnell's
    Funeral.'
    He is probably . . . his bardic sleep.'   /   Auden and Mac-
    Neice, *Letters from Iceland*, p. 242.
    There was MacKenna . . . flight of Mind,   /   MacNeice,
    'Eclogue from Iceland,' in *Letters from Iceland*, p. 131.
100–101. With Yeats . . . wandering stars')   /   Yeats, 'Who Goes
    with Fergus?'
101. while with Auden . . . buried engine-room.'   /   Auden,
    Poems (1928, private edition by Stephen Spender), p. 9.
    while Auden, disdaining . . . or extremely rare.'   /   Ibid.,
    pp. 18, 18, 6, 27.
    Nor speech . . . than it meant.   /   Ibid., p. 26.
    The necessary obverse . . . in thoughtless heaven.'   /
    Auden, *On This Island* (New York, 1937), p. 11.
101–2. 'It was not the fault . . . and poetic nature.'   /   Auden,
    'On "A Change of Air," ' in *The Contemporary Poet as
    Artist and Critic*, ed. Anthony Ostroff (Boston, 1964),
    p. 185.
102. He attributes to . . . the naked truth.'   /   Ibid.
    I, though a watcher . . . turn your head?   /   Auden,
    Poems (1928), p. 6.
    O heart! . . . folly of being comforted.   /   Yeats, 'The
    Folly of Being Comforted.'
    Another poem . . . Spender has noted,   /   Stephen
    Spender, 'The Influence of Yeats on Later English
    Poets,' *Tri-Quarterly* (No. 4) 84–85.
102–3. I choose . . . dripping stone,   /   Yeats, 'The Tower.'

103. I chose this ... unaccustomed lip ... / Auden, *Poems*
     (1928), p. 8.
105. Among them ... review of *Last Poems*, / Auden,
     'Yeats: Master of Diction,' 14.
     one is a mock-trial ... prosecution and defense. /
     Auden, 'The Public v. the Late Mr. William Butler
     Yeats,' *Partisan Review* VI.3 (Spring 1939) 46–51.
     Another is ... serious reflections themselves. / Auden,
     'Yeats as an Example,' *Kenyon Review* X.2 (Spring
     1948) 187–95.
     When he came ... *New Yorker*, / Auden, ' "I Am of
     Ireland," ' *New Yorker* XXXI.5 (19 March 1955) 142–
     50.
     But in reviewing *Mythologies* for a book club, / Auden,
     'The Private Life of a Public Man,' in *The Mid-Century*,
     No. 4 (October 1959) 8–15.
106. To get ... people he hates. / In 'Academic Graffiti,'
     Homage to Clio (1960), p. 90.
106–7. In the most recent version of the poem, / 'In Memory
     of W. B. Yeats,' *Collected Shorter Poems* 1927–1957
     (London, 1966), pp. 141–42.
107. between the peasantry and 'hard-riding country gentlemen,'
     / Yeats, 'Under Ben Bulben.'
108. In prose Auden ... 'not conspicuously intelligent,' /
     Auden, 'The Private Life of a Public Man,' p. 14.
     In the *New Republic*, where the first version ... / *New
     Republic* LXXXVIII (8 March 1939) 578–80.
     Now he is led ... inserted in the poem, / 'The Public
     v. the Late Mr. William Butler Yeats,' p. 51.
     In one of his essays ... opinions were unjust / Ibid.
109. Auden, described by Isherwood ... high church, / Isher-
     wood, *Lions and Shadows*, p. 182.
     looking out at ... 'Sligo in heaven.' / Ezra Pound,
     Canto 77 (p. 51 of *Pisan Cantos*).
     Auden has always ... Birmingham to Wolverhampton. /
     Auden and MacNeice, *Letters from Iceland*, p. 51.
     If Yeats ... pieces of machinery.' / Ibid.
     I'm not sure ... lead mines, / Ibid., p. 205; and cf. *The
     Dyer's Hand* (New York, 1962), p. 102.

110. —while Auden was ... to develop gills.' / Auden,
     Poems (1928), p. 36. Auden's first master was Thomas
     Hardy, see *The Dyer's Hand*, p. 38.

111. He complains ... believed by a gentleman.' / 'Yeats as
     an Example,' in *The Kenyon Critics*, ed. John Crowe
     Ransom (Cleveland and New York, 1951), p. 109.
     He calls Yeats's.... 'Southern Californian,' / Ibid.
     and elsewhere ... artistically formed. / Auden, 'The
     Private Life of a Public Man,' p. 13.
     It may be that Auden ... in pre-ordination, in Fate. /
     Igor Stravinsky and Robert Craft, *Memories and Com-
     mentaries* (New York, 1960), pp. 157–58.
     Auden disavows ... sanity and salvation.' / Letter to
     Ellmann, 20 April 1967.

112. Auden is usually chary ... structures which we call poems.'
     / Auden, 'The Public v. the Late Mr. William Butler
     Yeats,' p. 49.
     The intellect ... or of the work,' / Yeats, 'The Choice.'
     Auden comments: ... possible in neither.' / Auden,
     The Dyer's Hand, p. 19.

112–13. When Yeats asks, ... called "a story." ' / Ibid., p. 281.

113. When Yeats writes ... would be more likely. / Ibid.,
     p. 353.
     When Yeats remarks ... that made no sense?' / Ibid.,
     p. 43.
     That he is not ... 'We'll die anyway.' / In conversation.
     * But Yeats is ... beginning of that poem. / Suggested
     by Robert O'Clair.

114. a failure to choose the Word instead of just words, /
     'Caliban to the Audience,' *The Sea and the Mirror* in
     For the Time Being (London, 1945).
     He thinks Yeats prefers, ... indifferent to truth, /
     'Yeats: Master of Diction,' 14, 'The Private Life of a
     Public Man,' p. 13.
     Prince Hal, ... Shakespeare's ideal king. / *The Dyer's
     Hand*, pp. 187–92.
     He refuses to ... of a Town Clerk.' / Yeats, 'At Strat-
     ford-on-Avon,' May 1901, in *Essays and Introductions*,
     p. 105.

114–15. 'Shakespeare watched . . . with tragic irony.' / Ibid., p. 109.

115. 'If you call it anything . . . Eliot said. / Eliot, 'Preface' to *The Sacred Wood* (New York, 1964), p. viii.

In his essay, . . . naming hidden relationships. / Auden, 'Squares and Oblongs,' in *Poets at Work*, ed. Charles D. Abbott (New York, 1948), pp. 173, 171.

Elsewhere he calls . . . can be done perfectly.' / Auden, *New Year Letter* (London, 1941), p. 89.

Monroe Spears calls . . . special gifts. / Monroe Spears, *The Poetry of W. H. Auden* (New York, 1963), pp. 335–36.

Auden remains . . . self-enchantment and deception.' / Auden, 'Robert Frost,' in *The Dyer's Hand*, p. 338.

116. Auden characteristically . . . moonshine and daylight.' / Auden, *The Sea and the Mirror* in *For the Time Being*, p. 15.

At other points . . . Caliban can call 'unrectored chaos' / Ibid., p. 33.

and that art offers . . . 'Wholly Other Life' / Ibid., p. 58.

though he would reject . . . glory symbolise.' / Yeats, 'Among School Children.'

117. We can imagine . . . hold with this.' / Yeats, 'Pages from a Diary Written in Nineteen Hundred and Thirty,' *Explorations* (London, 1962), p. 333.

He said rather . . . the poet's shadow, / Yeats, 'The Symbolism of Poetry,' *Essays and Introductions*, p. 158.

and he meant . . . 'heavenly labials.' / Wallace Stevens, 'The Plot against the Giant.'

In fact, as his letters . . . see or hope?' / Yeats, *Letters*, p. 833.

117–18. Auden, momentarily . . . Clarendon imprint. / 'The Public v. the Late Mr. William Butler Yeats,' p. 47.

118. (Years afterwards . . . 'Cambridge school.') / Yeats, *Letters*, pp. 886, 833.

In his late play . . . 'sprung verse') / Ibid., pp. 844–46.

118. and in his last prose work, . . . available now to us. /
     Yeats, *On the Boiler*, in *Explorations*, p. 450.

     He understood . . . 'antiquated romantic stuff,' / Yeats,
     prologue to *The Death of Cuchulain*.

     With Auden prominently . . . they may be modern.' / 'A
     General Introduction for My Work,' *Essays and Intro-
     ductions*, p. 525.

118–19. Remembering that Auden . . . expect a counter-Renais-
     sance.' / Ibid., pp. 525–26.

119. But if Yeats . . . his own late image. / Yeats, 'The Wild
     Old Wicked Man.'

     The claim of being . . . of gay warty lads.' / Yeats, *Let-
     ters on Poetry from W. B. Yeats to Dorothy Wellesley*,
     p. 69.

     Nor would Yeats . . . the middle style, / Auden, *New
     Year Letter*, p. 24.

     or, as Marianne Moore . . . circumspectly audacious.' /
     Marianne Moore, 'W. H. Auden,' *Predilections* (Lon-
     don, 1956), p. 85.

     If Auden was suspicious . . . a happy ending. / Yeats,
     'Introduction' to *Oxford Book of Modern Verse*, p.
     xxxvii.

     His own preference, . . . rather than tragicomedy. / Ibid.

120. Auden would insist, . . . midwife to society,' / Auden,
     New Year Letter, p. 19.

     'When did the poets . . . in *The King's Threshold*. /
     Yeats, *The King's Threshold*, line 818.

121. In temerariously rejecting . . . sucked sugar-stick') /
     Yeats, *Letters*, p. 874.

     and Sean O'Casey's *The Silver Tassie* . . . 'anti-war propa-
     ganda'), / Ibid., p. 743.

     It expresses a more volcanic . . . falls in ruin. / Yeats,
     The King's Threshold, lines 185–86.

     Auden argues against Shelley . . . legislators of the world; /
     Auden, 'Squares and Oblongs,' in *Poets at Work*, p. 177.

122. he finds it in Yeats a bit 'literary'; / Auden, 'The Pri-
     vate Life of a Public Man,' p. 14.

     his own love poems, . . . 'half-humbug and half-true,' /
     Auden, 'Serenade.'

122. Yeats: I believe in the poet's ... poetry is magic. /
     Yeats, 'Magic,' *Essays and Introductions*, p. 28, and 'The
     Symbolism of Poetry,' ibid., pp. 158–59.

     Auden: Poetry is not magic ... and disintoxicate. /
     Auden, *The Dyer's Hand*, p. 27.

     Yeats: Truth is the dramatic ... poet as hero. / Yeats
     and Edwin John Ellis, *The Works of William Blake*
     (London, 1893), v. I, p. 241; Ellmann, *Yeats: The Man
     and The Masks*, p. 6.

     Auden: The poet no longer ... possibility. / Auden,
     The Enchafèd Flood (New York, 1950), p. 152.

123. Auden: All that is passé ... has come in. / Auden and
     MacNeice, *Letters from Iceland*, p. 25.

     Yeats: The whale is extinct ... gasping on the strand. /
     Yeats, 'A General Introduction for My Work,' *Essays
     and Introductions*, pp. 525–26; and his poem, 'The Three
     Movements.'

     Auden: The artist no longer ... in elections. / Auden,
     The Enchafèd Flood, p. 153; cf. his view of Shakespeare
     in *The Dyer's Hand*, pp. 182–90.

     Auden: You belong to the school ... out of nothing. /
     Auden, *The Dyer's Hand*, p. 76.

     Yeats: You belong to the school ... cutting edge. /
     Yeats, 'Fragments,' and his descriptions of phases 23 and
     24 in *A Vision*.

126. Auden might have ... verbal contraption.' / Auden,
     The Dyer's Hand, p. 50.

Index